EAL Section C
Units 3 & 4

First published in 2024
Insight Publications Pty Ltd
3/350 Charman Road
Cheltenham Victoria 3192
Australia

Tel: +61 3 8571 4950
Email: books@insightpublications.com.au

www.insightpublications.com.au

Insight VCE Revision Questions: EAL Section C Units 3 & 4

ISBN: 9781923154933

Cover design and internal layout by Melisa Paredes
Internal design by Bec Yule @ Red Chilli Design
Proofread by Janice Bird
Printed by Markono Print Media Pte Ltd

Insight Publications acknowledges the Traditional Custodians of the Country on which we meet and work, the Boonwurrung People of the Kulin Nation. We pay our respects to their Elders past and present, and extend that respect to all Aboriginal and Torres Strait Islander peoples.

Contents

Introduction

This *VCE Revision Questions: EAL Section C Units 3 & 4* resource contains a variety of scenarios consisting of persuasive media texts in different forms, together with background information about the text and the issue it addresses, similar to those you will encounter in the end-of-Year-12 EAL examination. Tips for analysing each scenario are also included. The second section of this resource presents a high-level sample analysis of each scenario. This resource complies with the 2024–2027 VCE EAL Study Design.

By using *VCE Revision Questions: EAL Section C Units 3 & 4* as part of your study regime throughout the year, you will be well prepared for the sorts of texts you may encounter in Section C of your end-of-year VCE EAL examination.

We wish you well with your studies.

The Insight Team

SCENARIOS

Scenario 1: Life skills in schools

Instructions

- In this section, you are required to analyse the use of argument(s) and language to persuade an intended audience to share the point of view expressed in an unseen persuasive text.
- Read the background information on this page and the material on the following pages, and write an analytical response to the task below.
- For the purposes of this task, the term 'language' refers to written and spoken language, and 'visuals' refers to images and graphics.
- This section is worth one-third of the total marks for the examination.

Task

Write an analysis of the ways in which argument(s), written and spoken language, and visuals are used in the material on the following pages to try to persuade the intended audience to share the point of view presented.

Background information

The Student Representative Council at Olympus High School has written an open letter to be circulated among Olympus High students, asking them to sign a petition. The council is seeking support from the student body to present the petition to the school board, requesting that dedicated classes on life skills be introduced at the school for students in Years 7–10.

Olympus High Student Representative Council needs your help!

Please sign our petition to show your support for the idea of dedicated life skills classes for Year 7–10 students.

Fellow students, something is wrong with our school system. Something is wrong when students know Pythagoras' theorem but don't know how to lodge a tax return. Something is wrong when students know that the mitochondria are the powerhouses of the cell but don't know how to manage conflict in their personal lives. The steps to the Nutbush[1] might be handy to know at weddings, but surely mindfulness strategies and ways to cope with stress would be handier to know as we make the transition from adolescence to adulthood.

Our teaching and learning program should be focusing on the skills we need to succeed, not only in the professional world but also in our personal lives, and the government agrees. Personal and social capability is part of the Australian Curriculum. Across all year levels and studies, it is expected that students will develop skills in self-management and relationship-building. These skills are designed to support students in becoming individuals who, as outlined in the Melbourne Declaration on Educational Goals for Young Australians, can 'manage their emotional, mental, spiritual and physical wellbeing [with] a sense of optimism about their lives [and who can] form and maintain healthy relationships'. The government recognises the importance of developing both resilience and the capacity for positive relationship-building in the next generation, so why doesn't Olympus High?

The expectation is that these skills will be taught across all study areas, but this is not happening. The school seems to think that setting group projects in science classes is enough to help us develop our communication and goal-setting skills, and that reading other people's work in history and English classes is enough to help us to develop empathy. But this is not enough. The Student Representative Council proposes that at least once per month a dedicated class be held focusing on the practical applications of these skills. The classes would be open to all students across Years 7–10 and could be held at lunchtime if scheduling was difficult.

Each class would be led by a teacher from a different study area. We would have arts and music classes that focus on mental, emotional and spiritual wellbeing and mindfulness. We would have mathematics classes devoted to financial literacy and budgeting. We would have health and physical education classes focused on physical activity as a form of stress relief.

Providing students with practical strategies for dealing with stress and anxiety, in particular, should be a priority for our school leaders. The latest youth mental health report from Mission Australia and the Black Dog Institute found that, in the last seven years, psychological distress has risen by 5.5% among young people, and almost one in four young people in this country is experiencing mental health challenges. There is hope, however. According to research conducted by the Black Dog Institute, over 75% of mental health issues develop before the age of 25, indicating that early intervention is key. These classes would therefore be an investment in our long-term mental and emotional wellbeing.

Parents also agree that life skills should be taught in school. A 2019 study undertaken by Deana Leahy and Neil Selwyn of Monash University showed that parents want their children to receive a more holistic education. Responses to the question 'What new learning areas do people think should be taught in public schools?' referenced money management, home loans and taxes; job preparation such as résumé writing and interviewing; domestic tasks such as laundry and cooking; and conflict de-escalation.

While some may argue that these are skills we should be learning at home from our parents, modern-day economic pressures mean that both parents are likely to be working full time. According to the Australian Bureau of Statistics, in over half of Australia's two-parent households, both parents worked full time in 2020. Parents' roles and responsibilities have changed in recent times, but our school system has not kept up. Our parents need support in passing on the skills necessary for us to thrive in the adult world.

So please, if you agree that Olympus students deserve to be given the best possible opportunity to succeed after high school, sign our petition and ask your parents to do so too. The school board meets next month. Let's try to get at least 100 signatures!

[1]**Nutbush** – a type of dance

Tips

- » The exclamatory headline aims to immediately catch readers' attention and position them to feel that they have something of value to offer in this debate, encouraging them to read on. Look for ways in which this kind of direct appeal is continued in the body of the text.
- » Consider the text type – a petition – and intended audience – the writer's fellow students. The use of direct address – 'you' – and inclusive language – 'us', 'our' – aims to emphasise the shared interests of the writer and readers in order to get them on side.
- » Humour is also used to engage the audience; for example in the reference to 'the steps to the Nutbush' and the image of shapes, which is similar to shareable online memes. These would seem familiar to students, helping them to feel that the issue is relevant to their lives and that engaging with it will be as easy as their everyday interactions on social media.
- » Note that these humorous elements appear early in the piece, to develop a rapport with the reader from the beginning. Having done so, the writer shifts to a more serious tone to present evidence and research.
- » The text opens and closes with a statement that directly addresses readers. This both helps to create a sense of urgency in relation to the issue and positions readers to feel that they can and should act to support a change at their school.

Scenario 2: Greenwashing

Instructions

- In this section, you are required to analyse the use of argument(s) and language to persuade an intended audience to share the point of view expressed in an unseen persuasive text.
- Read the background information on this page and the material on the following pages, and write an analytical response to the task below.
- For the purposes of this task, the term 'language' refers to written and spoken language, and 'visuals' refers to images and graphics.
- This section is worth one-third of the total marks for the examination.

Task

Write an analysis of the ways in which argument(s), written and spoken language, and visuals are used in the material on the following pages to try to persuade the intended audience to share the point of view presented.

Background information

Makena Green-Moore is an environmental shopper and ethical consumerism advocate. The following is a transcript of her presentation at an expo on ethical consumerism. The presentation was accompanied by supporting images, and two of these images are included with the transcript.

Hello everyone. It is my great pleasure to welcome you all to today's presentation on ethical consumerism[1]. Thank you so much for being here.

First, I would like to acknowledge the Wurundjeri People of the Kulin Nation as the Traditional Owners of the land we are meeting on. I would like to pay my respects to the Elders, past and present.

To get us started I'd like everyone to close their eyes and picture this: you are in the supermarket, and you need to buy a new shampoo. While looking at the rack you see that a big sticker has been added to the front of an already familiar bottle: 'ALL NATURAL INGREDIENTS'. Fantastic, you think: now you can satisfy your need for shampoo and also buy something great for the environment.

WRONG!

You have just been subjected to 'greenwashing' or 'green sheen': an unethical marketing strategy designed to make you believe you are buying an eco-conscious product, when actually the company is not putting in the money, time and effort to create something environmentally friendly.

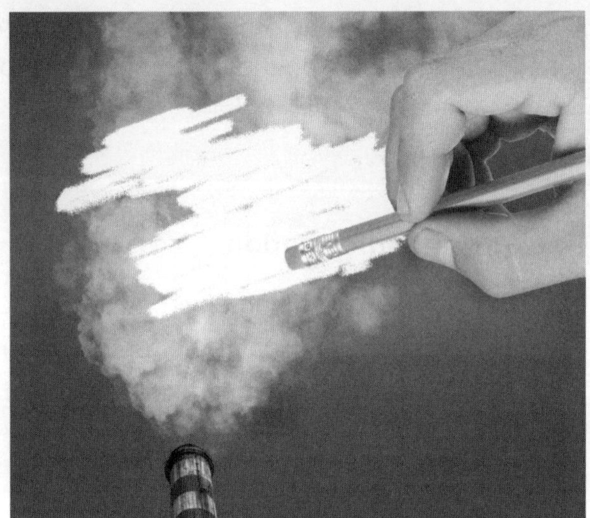

Greenwashing can take many forms, and specialised language has been created by clever manufacturers and marketers to convince consumers that they are making a more ethical choice than they truly are.

'All natural' is a common phrase thrown around by greenwashing marketers. This vague term implies an eco-friendliness without actually having to deliver on making a product environmentally beneficial. Think about it: most things are naturally occurring in some way, but that doesn't necessarily mean that they are good for you or good for the planet. Other terms often used include 'non-toxic', 'raw' and 'plant-based'. Not one of these descriptions guarantees any kind of environmental protection or benefit. Some companies have also created false labels or symbols that imply that they care about our cause. For example, a small green flower positioned on the bottom of the label can look deceptively similar to the real and well-known symbols that denote products being cruelty-free and recyclable.

The great news is that many of the companies who are well known for greenwashing are being called out and held accountable.

The Earth Island Institute recently filed a lawsuit against Coca-Cola for falsely advertising its products as eco-friendly while the company remains the largest plastic polluter in the world. The lawsuit was a retaliation against Coke's revelation that the bottles were being made with 'plant plastic' – an announcement attempting to sell the idea that the packaging would break down more easily than ever before. However, this misses the point entirely. Plant-based plastic is still plastic, and it is an unnecessary product when the more sustainable alternatives of glass and aluminium already exist.

Beware the label – a popular form of greenwashing.

What's great about this is that Coca-Cola is already being taken to court over its misleading marketing, and now there will be real pressure on the company to genuinely reduce the environmental impact of its packaging.

Of course, that is an example of dealing with greenwashing on a large and extremely expensive scale – not all of us can afford to take on a giant company in a legal battle.

So, what easy changes can we make to our own shopping habits to ensure we aren't falling for these nasty tactics?

As I mentioned earlier, pay careful attention to the terminology being used on packaging; think about what terms like 'all natural' really mean, and ensure you know what the real eco-friendly symbols look like. Pictures of nature, greenery and flowers will often be used but do not represent official approval. If you are concerned that the producers of your favourite products aren't being honest with you, reach out to them and ask for the truth. You can find the contact details for brands online, so get in touch and tell them your concerns. If you get a vague response then they probably have nothing positive to say. It might be difficult to say goodbye to a much-loved favourite, but there are many great ethical products out there for you to try.

If you can, try to buy local alternatives – a farmers' market is a great place to buy produce direct from the people who make it, usually with minimal or no packaging. Ultimately, with a little bit of extra knowledge, a keen eye and the will to do what is right, we can make many small changes in our lives that will all add up to a more environmentally friendly and sustainable community.

Thank you all again for your attendance today. I'll be around the expo for a while so please feel free to approach me if you have any questions about ethical consuming or greenwashing, or even if you'd just like to say hello. And remember – don't let the big corporations trick you!

[1]**consumerism** – the acquisition and/or consumption of goods and resources

Tips

- In your analysis, it is especially important to take into account the context of this text. The speaker is addressing an audience of people who will probably be receptive to her message, since they are attending an ethical consumerism expo. She can assume they care for the environment and therefore she can focus on ways in which they can do this most effectively.
- The speaker repeatedly addresses the audience directly, using 'you'; this both retains her listeners' attention and helps her to foster a connection between them and herself.
- Look for other ways the speaker aims to develop this connection – for example, through her invitation to 'please feel free to approach me', which helps to create an impression of friendliness and transparency.
- The inclusion of the Acknowledgement of Country at the beginning of the speech further reinforces the speaker's ethical credentials, contributing to an image of her as informed and concerned with social justice issues, an impression likely to be well received by this particular audience.
- Though the speaker's aim is to alert her audience to greenwashing tactics, she is careful not to put listeners offside by suggesting that they are foolish or ignorant to believe manufacturers' claims about environmental friendliness. By referring to 'clever' marketers and manufacturers, whose tactics are 'unethical' and 'nasty', she places the blame for greenwashing on organisations, rather than on consumers themselves. This allows her audience to feel that her advice will give them an advantage when it comes to assessing companies' environmental claims, rather than positioning them to feel that they should feel guilty if they have previously fallen for the sorts of false claims she criticises.

Scenario 3: Highfield Markets

Instructions

- In this section, you are required to analyse the use of argument(s) and language to persuade an intended audience to share the point of view expressed in an unseen persuasive text.
- Read the background information on this page and the material on the following pages, and write an analytical response to the task below.
- For the purposes of this task, the term 'language' refers to written and spoken language, and 'visuals' refers to images and graphics.
- This section is worth one-third of the total marks for the examination.

Task

Write an analysis of the ways in which argument(s), written and spoken language, and visuals are used in the material on the following pages to try to persuade the intended audience to share the point of view presented.

Background information

Highfield Discussions is a podcast that addresses community issues in the Highfield area. In this episode, Ravi Nicholson expresses his views on the proposed loss of the local markets, with the intended replacement being a large supermarket. The transcript was published on the *Highfield Discussions* website, as well as on relevant social media platforms, accompanied by two images.

Hello to you all, I hope you're having a great day. You're probably wondering why you're hearing from me again so soon. I'm making this episode as a bit of a bonus feature; something has come to my attention, and I really couldn't sit on it until next week. I think, at this point, we all know how passionate I am about our community. Obviously, Highfield has seen a lot of change recently, and most of it has been fantastic. The new local pool is a great addition, I've loved the green spaces being used for morning yoga, and the street veggie patch has contributed to more than my fair share of meals. But … I was absolutely heartbroken to find out yesterday that there are talks of demolishing the Highfield Markets. I've been running around those stalls since I was five; it's always been such an open, safe space. As kids we would weave between stands, sheltering from the sun under colourful umbrellas before launching into a new game. If we fell? Not to worry – plenty of friendly faces were around to provide a pat on the back, a bandaid and an icy pole for good measure. Even now as an adult I'm happy to say that my children run around just as we all did then. So, I got to thinking about the proposed demolition. Is it for a new structure? Are they revamping the markets? Are they moving them and making room for a new community feature?

I'll let you know now, it's none of the above. They want to demolish the markets to make room for a new supermarket. Just another chain store in a big concrete block. To me, and many others, this would be an unthinkable loss. I can understand it; our recent community upgrades make this a very desirable and well-serviced location and we have had an influx of new neighbours – which is great! I'm not surprised we have been put on the map, and if the developers had been able to find an empty space to fill, I don't think anyone would mind. But this comes at the cost of the families and small businesses that have worked out of and relied on these markets for decades. Our local economy is at stake, and the work and wellbeing of beloved community members is being undermined. Even beyond this, the produce and goods that will be supplied by this supermarket won't be able to compare with the high-quality fresh products that we are used to.

I don't know about you, but I don't want another lifeless supermarket chain arriving at the expense of small businesses that provide our community with a heartbeat. Demolishing the markets threatens not only our local economy but also a core pillar of our community. So much of what makes Highfield special can be found at the markets. I couldn't imagine a Sunday morning without a coffee from Letitia's stand, fresh fruit from Manuel's, and Francois' fresh bread. It is these businesses – these people – who will suffer if this moves forward.

Ultimately, I care more about the livelihood of the families and their independent businesses than I do about the profit margins of a big developer. These supermarket chains clearly haven't considered the amount of community support for local enterprises. By shopping at the supermarket, we would be sending the profits outside of our community, giving the supermarkets money that they won't be putting back into our local economy. The markets are not only an economic backbone of our community, but also a social one, and I say this because I KNOW that Highfield supports me.

To my listeners, I'm asking you to consider what you can do to keep Highfield safe. Many of you will already have seen the protest posters and signs around the markets and I applaud those who created these for taking action so quickly. I also have the 'Protect Highfield Markets' petition link in the episode description, and I would really love to see more people get involved in this important issue. Write to your local councillor and make your feelings known.

Most of all, head down to the markets this weekend and every weekend and support the businesses that are still there. Each one of them desperately needs us to demonstrate how essential they are to our community. You can do this while also getting some great produce. Highfield is a community that cares for each other during the hard times, so please support what makes us special and protest against what will make us ordinary.

Next week we will be back to our regular programming, so thanks for listening and remember to shop local!

Tips

- Consider how the opening of the text prepares listeners to view the issue as both urgent and relevant, as the speaker makes the point that this is a 'bonus feature' that he couldn't 'sit on' for another week. This opening also treats listeners as a community that is well acquainted with the podcast and its host, strengthening a pre-existing rapport.
- Note the way in which the two images are intended to work in tandem by presenting two starkly contrasting views of the market site – one in which the area is bustling and vibrant, and one in which it is almost empty and seems desolate. This contrast reinforces the one conveyed in the spoken text, between the popular markets that foster a sense of community and the proposed supermarket development that the speaker argues will undermine it.
- The speaker repeatedly frames the supermarket development as a threat through careful language choices with connotations of harm and destruction, such as 'demolish', 'lifeless' and 'suffer'. Look for other examples, and consider the emotions being targeted by this vocabulary.
- Contrast these negative vocabulary choices with the descriptions of the current markets – e.g. 'open', 'safe', 'high-quality fresh products', 'heartbeat'. Such choices work to establish the market as vital to the community, positioning listeners to feel that the proposed development threatens not only a familiar place to shop but their wellbeing and safety, as well as their sense of community.
- Consider the way Nicholson creates a connection with his audience by repeatedly addressing them directly throughout his podcast. The medium of the podcast allows the speaker to build this sort of rapport with his audience, and the use of direct address also helps him to personalise the issue.

Scenario 4: Handwriting

Instructions

- In this section, you are required to analyse the use of argument(s) and language to persuade an intended audience to share the point of view expressed in an unseen persuasive text.
- Read the background information on this page and the material on the following pages, and write an analytical response to the task below.
- For the purposes of this task, the term 'language' refers to written and spoken language, and 'visuals' refers to images and graphics.
- This section is worth one-third of the total marks for the examination.

Task

Write an analysis of the ways in which argument(s), written and spoken language, and visuals are used in the material on the following pages to try to persuade the intended audience to share the point of view presented.

Background information

The following opinion piece by Leslie Slater appeared in a magazine supplement to a weekend newspaper. It is her response to discussions about the increasing use of computer technology, particularly in education, and the implications for handwriting.

The vanishing art of handwriting

By Leslie Slater

It was only a couple of years ago that I discovered the pleasures of using a fountain pen. The way each stroke of a letter can be subtly varied, depending on the angle and pressure with which the nib is placed on the page. The way the colour of the ink gradually changes as it dries. And yes, the way the letters smudge if my hand rests on the drying ink: a sign of imperfection and vulnerability; a mirror held up to their human creator. From being a purely functional task, writing has now taken on a more creative quality, and I have an enhanced awareness of how *what* I write is connected to *how* I write it.

Then there are the environmental benefits: no more disposable pens going into landfill. A bottle of ink lasts a long time, and the glass can be recycled. Even the refill process can be enjoyable, as the pen is first flushed carefully with water and then ink is drawn up. The variety of ink colours available is far greater than the narrow range of standard colours in disposable pens, encompassing shades of pink, amber, coffee, grey, violet and everything in between.

Beautiful handwriting: a vanishing art?

I am not the only one who appreciates the act of handwriting, especially (though not exclusively) with bottled ink and fountain pen. The book *The Missing Ink: The Lost Art of Handwriting (and Why it Still Matters)* by Philip Hensher also celebrates the pleasures of handwriting. For Hensher, handwriting is not just a way to give someone information, but an expression of the individual that incorporates 'a little bit of their personality into the form of their message'. In other words, handwriting is essentially personal and unique rather than mechanical and mass-produced.

Yet at this moment in history, the future of handwriting is suddenly extremely uncertain. As Hensher admits, he wrote his book at a time 'when, it seems, handwriting is about to vanish from our lives altogether'. Computers, tablets and smart phones mean we are, as never before, finger-tapping at keyboards and keypads rather than deliberately shaping each stroke and curve of letters and punctuation marks. For a culture to lose handwriting is, perhaps, also to lose part of its history, its identity, even its humanity.

Of course, handwriting is still taught in Australian primary schools. But typing on laptops and other devices is the vastly more common way in which students produce written work, meaning that secondary school students are left to find their own preferred way of handwriting – on the rare occasions when they still need to. Then they somehow have to overcome the challenge of writing their exams, which can be up to three hours long in Year 12. Experienced English and Literature teacher Kim Jones notes that many senior students resort to printing and even block capital letters, which can mean they struggle in a written exam. 'Some students find it too physically difficult as the muscles in their hands and fingers become sore and fatigued. They don't write as much as they should and they may fail to complete all their answers.' It seems just a matter of time before all exams will be undertaken electronically. Once that happens there will be little or no reason for students to handwrite beyond their early primary school years, with the resulting loss of those skills acquired in the first 11 or 12 years of life. The writing, as they say, is on the wall.

Is it only old-fashioned people like me who will mourn the loss of handwriting? Is it just about aesthetics – about something *looking* beautiful, but lacking much use or meaning? Or an empty nostalgia about how it was in the 'old days'? And anyway, what exactly *does* poor or immaculate handwriting say about the individual – about, for instance, their personal qualities or values? We don't make assumptions about someone's personality purely on the basis of their skill in athletics or ball sports. Perhaps handwriting says nothing much at all about us, and doing it much less, or not at all, does not compromise our intelligence or our humanity.

Students almost exclusively complete assignments electronically nowadays.

Yet there is a growing body of evidence that suggests we do, somehow, think *differently*, and perhaps *better*, when we handwrite than when we type. In a US study reported on the University of Washington website, professor of educational psychology Virginia Berninger and her colleagues compared how 200 students in grades 2, 4 and 6 completed writing tasks using a pen and using a keyboard. 'Children consistently did better writing with a pen when they wrote essays,' says Berninger. 'They wrote more and they wrote faster.' Although it is far from clear why this might be, Berninger suggests that 'a keyboard doesn't allow a child to have the same opportunity to engage the hand while forming letters – on a keyboard a letter is selected by pressing a key and is not formed.' She adds, 'Brain imaging studies with adults have shown an advantage for forming letters over selecting or viewing letters.'

Another study found that adults learning a new (foreign) alphabet by hand scored better in recognition tests than those learning the alphabet using a keyboard and screen. When brain scans were performed, those who learned by hand showed more activity in the part of the brain that controls language comprehension. In other words, the way we write affects the way we learn. And the way we learn affects … well, just about everything.

All of which suggests we should be concerned about the shift away from pen and paper. What gifts handwriting may have for us may not be fully understood until it's too late – when handwriting is no longer part of the curriculum (as in many states in the US), and when teachers lack the knowledge of how to teach it because they haven't learned it themselves. The information age is here, and it's essentially a digital, computer age with great liberating and democratic potential. But that doesn't mean that we can't also keep what's valuable, unique and often beautiful from the past. Handwriting is not only a vital part of our heritage; it may also be a crucial part of our minds.

Tips

» Note the way in which Slater balances emotional appeals to aesthetics and nostalgia with logical, evidence-based arguments regarding the usefulness of handwriting to memory and learning. How might this help her appeal to a wide and diverse audience?

» Slater bolsters her argument with references to expert testimony; these are varied yet all relevant to the field of education, thus providing strong evidence in support of her opinion. Referring to both Australian and international evidence implies that the writer's research is wide-ranging and her conclusions thus more reliable. It also suggests that the issue is globally significant, inclining the reader to feel that something important is at stake.

» The writer uses an often lyrical tone, particularly in the opening and closing paragraphs. Identify particular language choices that contribute to this tone and reflect on how it supports her two-pronged argument about the value of handwriting.

» Consider the importance of the place of publication of this piece. Its appearance in a supplementary weekend magazine means that readers are likely to consume it in a more leisurely, thoughtful way than they might a piece published in the main daily news section of the newspaper. Thus the writer's considered meditations on the issue are likely to be received in a similarly considered manner by her audience.

» Note the two images included with the article: the first, a close-up of a handwritten note, illustrates the writer's view regarding the beauty of handwriting. The image centres on a sleek fountain pen which, in tandem with the caption, encourages readers to see for themselves the beauty of traditional handwriting. The second is framed from a first-person perspective, which invites the reader to place themselves in the position of the student. The crumpled paper represents the metaphorical discarding of physical implements such as pen and paper, and suggests a sense of frustration compared to the emphasis on beauty in the first image.

Scenario 5: Penny's Petals

Instructions

- In this section, you are required to analyse the use of argument(s) and language to persuade an intended audience to share the point of view expressed in an unseen persuasive text.
- Read the background information on this page and the material on the following pages, and write an analytical response to the task below.
- For the purposes of this task, the term 'language' refers to written and spoken language, and 'visuals' refers to images and graphics.
- This section is worth one-third of the total marks for the examination.

Task

Write an analysis of the ways in which argument(s), written and spoken language, and visuals are used in the material on the following pages to try to persuade the intended audience to share the point of view presented.

Background information

Penelope Acosta is the owner of the local flower shop Penny's Petals. She has written a blog post about what inspired her to start her business, and the ethics of the modern cut-flower business. She has shared this post on her social media pages.

Shock in the shop! The ethics of cut flowers

By Penelope Acosta

A rose by any other name would smell as sweet – but where did that rose come from?

This was the question I asked myself ten years ago when receiving a beautiful bouquet for my 30th birthday. Roses were my favourite flower, but surely it was the wrong time of year for such a gorgeous display. How were these flowers in bloom in autumn?

Thus, my search started, and I was shocked to find out that the roses I so adored had a far more sinister background than I ever could have imagined.

The modern flower industry is fraught with difficulty, exploitation and environmentally dangerous practices. With the global cut-flower industry being worth an estimated US$55 billion, the majority of flowers are being imported from South America and East Asia. Colombia leads all other flower producers, having sold 660 million stems during 2020. The plants on these flower farms are grown in industrial-scale greenhouses that can occupy more than 200 hectares. Here the workers can be expected to work 16-hour days. Further, although floriculture[1] exposes workers to fertilisers, insecticides and preservatives that are absolutely full of toxins, employees are often expected to work without personal protective equipment. Despite taking these risks, the workers are paid far below the minimum wage, hardly able to support themselves and their families.

Just when I thought this couldn't get worse, I found that it is not only the workers who are affected, but also the communities surrounding these unscrupulous flower farms. In Ecuador, young children who come into contact with floriculture workers have been assessed for altered short-term brain activity that is suspected to be a result of contamination from pesticide residue on clothes and equipment.

Everything I have mentioned so far is shocking enough, but it doesn't even consider the environmental toll this industry can take. The masses of stems being grown on flower farms need vast quantities of water, putting a huge strain on local resources. Once these flowers have been harvested, they are distributed all over the world, leaving an astronomical carbon footprint in their wake. Finally, once in store at the florist or supermarket, they are wrapped in harsh plastics and shoved onto foam blocks that are laced with chemicals and virtually impossible to recycle or dispose of ethically.

I couldn't see how I could keep enjoying a birthday bouquet with all of this new knowledge. How could I be sure that the flowers I was buying were ethically sourced and sustainably grown?

So, I started my own florist shop. Ten years on, I am proud to say that the flowers I sell at Penny's Petals aren't grown using any of these dangerous methods, and anyone buying from our shop can be sure that I take the greatest care with my work.

My first intention with every bloom is to attempt to grow it myself. I have a small local farm, where I grow my beautiful Australian natives. I also have a greenhouse that I use for my harder-to-grow crops – but I take care not to overuse water or chemicals. My family and I carefully attend to each and every plant, using only the most eco-friendly and sustainable of products.

If I can't find a way to produce the flowers myself, I make the effort to source my flowers from Aussie farmers, who I know take the time to nurture strong and beautiful plants while minimising the use of water and toxic chemicals. I also have the added pleasure of supporting Australian businesses just like mine. Penny's Petals doesn't use foam blocks or plastics; we wrap our flowers in recyclable materials and, where possible, we supply a second-hand vase to keep your beautiful arrangements blooming for longer.

The next time you are in a mad dash to impress, or say sorry, or buy that 'just because' bouquet, forget the big chains. Sure, they might save you a few dollars, but you are overlooking the real cost of those stems.

[1]**floriculture** – an industry that produces and cultivates flowers, especially for show

Tips

- Be alert to the dual purpose of the blog post – to dissuade the reader from purchasing flowers that are not ethically produced and to promote the writer's own florist business in order to increase sales.
- This double purpose leads Acosta to create a dichotomy between irresponsible, unethical 'big chain' flower-sellers on the one hand and ethical business on the other. Note, however, that the ethical practices she describes all relate to her own business, thus implying that the best or only option for the responsible consumer is to purchase from Penny's Petals.
- Acosta makes frequent use of highly emotive language, such as 'shocking', 'dangerous' and 'sinister', which work together to develop a strongly negative portrayal of traditional florists and aim to evoke fear, sympathy and outrage in the reader.
- She also uses extreme language, such as 'astronomical' and 'virtually impossible', which intensifies her use of emotive terms to convey an impression of the situation as dire and therefore requiring urgent action.
- Throughout the piece, Acosta frequently alludes to her personal knowledge of and interactions with the flower industry. She attempts to portray herself as an expert with extensive experience relevant to the topic. She also attempts to frame herself as an unsuspecting victim of unethical business practices, further lending her credibility as someone who has been exposed to the modern flower industry's issues. Consider how the context of the post's publication (on Acosta's social media and blog) might make her target audience more likely to accept her claims of authority.

Scenario 6: The wearable workplace

Instructions

- In this section, you are required to analyse the use of argument(s) and language to persuade an intended audience to share the point of view expressed in an unseen persuasive text.
- Read the background information on this page and the material on the following pages, and write an analytical response to the task below.
- For the purposes of this task, the term 'language' refers to written and spoken language, and 'visuals' refers to images and graphics.
- This section is worth one-third of the total marks for the examination.

Task

Write an analysis of the ways in which argument(s), written and spoken language, and visuals are used in the material on the following pages to try to persuade the intended audience to share the point of view presented.

Background information

The article below was published in *SuitNoTie*, an online publication for business executives who want to keep up with the latest trends and developments in the business world. Forsythe is a staff writer at *SuitNoTie* and he is the former CEO of a multinational company.

The wearable workplace

By Brannigan Forsythe

It's official – the wearable technology revolution is here, and there's plenty of room for businesses to get in on the action. From managing employee health to improving overall productivity, companies around the globe are using wearables to supercharge their operations, and there's no reason you can't do the same. Curious? We show you why now is the time to start thinking about working wearables into your world.

You can't put a price on health – or can you?

A quick survey of wearable tech on the market right now will tell you two things: one, wearables are more popular than ever; and two, they're predominantly pitched at the health conscious (or those trying to be).

Being health-conscious – getting your steps in, measuring the distance you run each morning – is great, but what does that have to do with you and your business?

There are plenty of reasons why health and fitness should be a company concern as well as a personal one. Research tells us that fitter and healthier employees have higher energy levels, are less likely to get sick and are more productive in the long term.

But getting your workers to take responsibility for improving their health is not so easy, especially as many employers are reluctant to order their employees to do so.

Enter wearables. As many companies can tell you, encouraging employees to use wearable tech like a Fitbit is a great way to foster greater health consciousness in your workplace, and the cost for the company is relatively small.

After all, what would you prefer to be paying for? A fitness tracker – which is getting cheaper by the day – or the cost of covering sick leave?

Wearables that work for you

Sickness and injury are simply an unpleasant reality that workplaces have to deal with, but there's no doubt that the incidence can vary from industry to industry.

When it comes to retail and manufacturing, the risk (and cost) can be crippling. US insurance company Liberty Mutual estimated the direct cost of overexertion injuries in these areas to be US$15.1 billion (one-quarter of the total workplace injury direct costs), and there's no reason to think that the proportion of costs in Australia would be significantly different.

Would activity trackers stop your workers getting injured on the job? Probably not, but there are a range of other wearable options out there – with some very impressive applications.

Step inside an Audi assembly plant, for example, and you'll be greeted by some of the world's first robotic workers. The German car maker has been trialling the use of wearable exoskeletons to reduce the stress on workers' bodies. Worn like a piece of clothing, the exoskeleton connects at the hips and features support structures across specific points on the upper and lower body.

Wearables also offer a number of benefits when it comes to responding to on-the-job accidents. Though not as complex as an exoskeleton, tech like Wearsafe is set to dramatically improve safety in high-risk environments.

Wearsafe is a wearable tag that can be activated with the push of a button in an emergency, automatically contacting first responders and supervisors with location data and real-time audio from the incident. It's a deceptively simple tech solution to an age-old problem – knowing where your workers are, what they're doing and when they get into trouble – and another example of wearable tech's revolutionary potential.

But there's more to this picture than physical fitness and safety. As any human resources manager will tell you, poor mental health is just as much of a drain on productivity as physical injury. The problem for those in management, however, is how to identify mental health issues early on.

Well, good news, folks! There's a wearable for that.

Take a look at multinational[1] company Hitachi, which has been trialling wearable sensors that collect and analyse data on employee behaviour to improve happiness. The state-of-the-art tech, embedded into what looks like a regular worker ID, tracks an employee's activities throughout the day to measure their levels of job satisfaction. The data is then analysed to highlight areas that management can improve upon to keep workers happy and, therefore, more productive.

Hitachi is not alone. Companies all over the world are using similar tech to measure employees' heart rates, as well as their fatigue and stress levels, to determine when they might be in need of a break (or a little more incentive!).

Working out what fits (and wearing the consequences)

Okay, you might now be convinced about the value of bringing wearables into the workplace, but be warned – it's not going to be such an easy sell to your employees.

With privacy concerns around technology use a high priority for many people, the prospect of employers collecting data on workers is likely to be met with some resistance. A recent survey by PricewaterhouseCoopers found that 82 per cent of respondents were concerned about the privacy implications of wearable tech, with many voicing concerns about the kinds of data collected, who would have access to it and what it might be used for.

The real issue, then, is trust, and the decision to implement wearable tech should come with a comprehensive plan for educating employees about how they will be affected and what processes are in place to protect their information.

That being said, it's clear that wearables are here to stay (they're not wearing out!), and keen CEOs need to keep ahead of the curve – or watch the revolution pass them by.

[1]**multinational** – operates in multiple countries

Tips

- Consider how the identity of the writer of the opinion piece might affect the way the audience responds to his point of view. The background information suggests that he is experienced and knowledgeable in the field, inclining the reader to trust his opinion. This authoritative status is also suggested by his use of statistics and references to high-profile multinational companies in his examples.
- Consider how the predominant tone of the article is likely to affect the audience. It is upbeat and positive, and reflects a professionalism appropriate to the context in which the piece appears. This is intended to evoke feelings of trust and positivity in the audience, which is likely to consist of businesspeople eager to find out about ways to increase productivity in their workplaces. Appealing to their desire to be modern and up to date, the writer uses motivational expressions such as 'keep ahead of the curve' that this audience is likely to be familiar with and find compelling.
- The structure of the piece further caters to the specific target audience with subheadings that highlight key points for readers who might not have the time or inclination to read the text from start to finish. It is also reminiscent of the structure of a workplace report of the sort readers are likely to be familiar with, and inclined to view as reliable and meaningful.
- Analyse the way the image presents an alternative viewpoint to that expressed in the opinion piece in order to rebut it. The cartoon depicts an employee who is clearly stressed, as indicated by the beads of sweat around his face as he runs. His wearable device is telling him that he is fired, which might be read as suggesting that such technology has excessive power over employees' lives. However, the exaggerated and comical nature of the illustration, together with the context of its appearance with the written piece undercuts any alarm the image might evoke. Rather the unlikelihood of an employee being fired by a wearable device operates to convey the idea that concern about wearable devices in the workplace is exaggerated and even ridiculous.

Scenario 7: Halloween

Instructions

- In this section, you are required to analyse the use of argument(s) and language to persuade an intended audience to share the point of view expressed in an unseen persuasive text.
- Read the background information on this page and the material on the following pages, and write an analytical response to the task below.
- For the purposes of this task, the term 'language' refers to written and spoken language, and 'visuals' refers to images and graphics.
- This section is worth one-third of the total marks for the examination.

Task

Write an analysis of the ways in which argument(s), written and spoken language, and visuals are used in the material on the following pages to try to persuade the intended audience to share the point of view presented.

Background information

The *Redfern Reader*, a free suburban newspaper, has a regular opinion column for members of the community to share their thoughts on local events. Recently there has been an influx of letters about Halloween and trick-or-treating. Local Redfern resident Nadia Laghari has written an opinion piece for the column, sharing her thoughts on the celebration.

Halloween – treat or trick? A personal journey

By Nadia Laghari

Well, it's that time of year again. Decorations are popping up everywhere, pumpkins are appearing in front yards (and in the veggie aisle!) and the kids seem to be more excited with every day. It's too early for Christmas, and we've just had school holidays – it must be Halloween.

It's taken me a long time to understand why we bother with Halloween. We already have so much American influence in our culture – movies, TV shows, music – without adopting one of their celebrations as well. I've often thought I'd prefer some kind of Australian festival on that day, rather than something with no local relevance. And as it stands, I don't love a ritual centred on the mass consumption of lollies. It's hard enough to encourage my kids to eat healthily without this sugary occasion on the calendar. Not to mention the havoc it brings to the dinnertime schedule. Halloween frequently falls on a school night, and dinner and bedtime are put on hold until whenever the kids are back from trick-or-treating. There's also the need to juggle getting the older kids to and from sports training, and running to the door every few minutes to dole out lollies to a never-ending stream of strangers. Then there are the yearly demands for new plastic costumes that just end up in the back of the cupboard, or even in the bin. While I would hate my kids to feel left out because they're not dressed in a great outfit, the thought of so much waste makes my head spin.

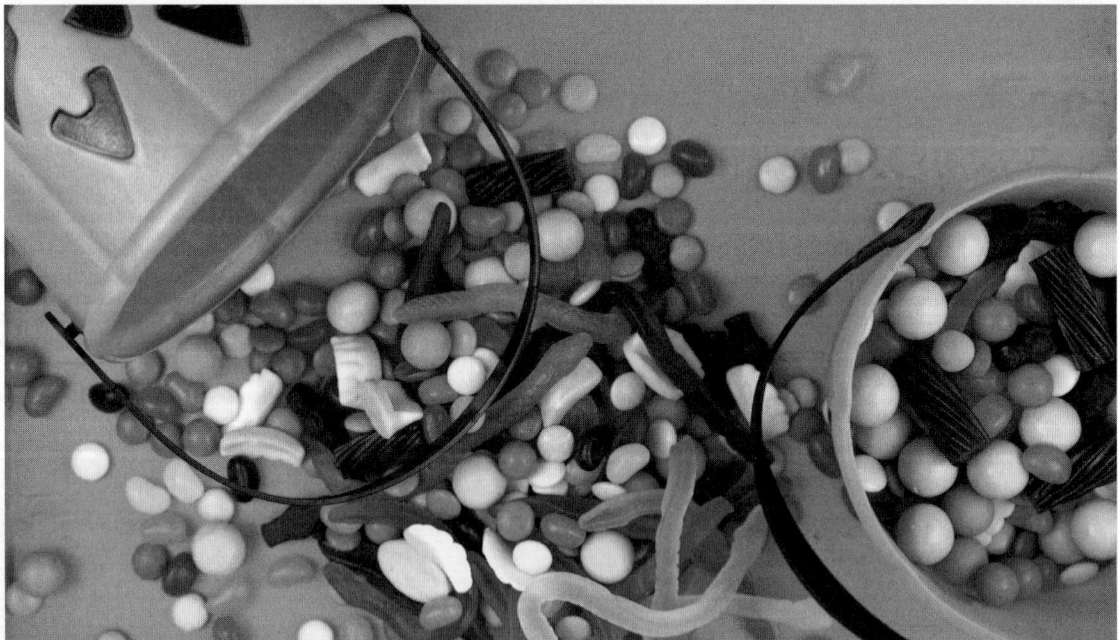

These used to be my first thoughts each October as I dreaded that haunted night. But over the years, seeing how much fun the kids have in their costumes with their friends, the life it brings to the street, and, yes, even sneaking a few lollies throughout the night myself, has gradually encouraged me to rethink Halloween. It didn't happen overnight, but by making an effort and getting more involved, I now find that I don't just tolerate Halloween – I enjoy it.

Seeing how the community makes Halloween its own on 31 October, I've grown to like the occasion. Plastic-wrapped candy is often replaced with home-baked cookies and fruit from the community garden. We've taken to giving out trail mix pouches to try and strike a balance of naughty and nice. We get a chance to say hello to neighbours we've fallen out of touch with, and meet the new families who have made this suburb their home in the past year. Seeing the street come to life with kids and adults alike dressed up and laughing has become a real highlight of my year. While we sometimes have street parties or get-togethers at other times, an event that includes the whole suburb feels really special.

It's also given me a chance to turn some of my worries into active opportunities to have fun with my kids, and even to impart some lessons. While, before, I might have been worried about their costumes being bought that morning and thrown away 24 hours later, now we see the costume challenge as an opportunity to imaginatively repurpose old clothes that might otherwise never get worn again. Not only does this give them a chance to actually practise reusing and recycling, it's creative and lets us bond over sticky tape and craft glue. It's also a great opportunity to see what they've been reading and watching, and which characters they like enough to want to dress up as. It's even inspired me to participate – I have a bit of a costume in the works this year!

I used to push back against a celebration that was so clearly imported, but then, so are Christmas and Easter, and we certainly enjoy those. The calendar is full of rituals that didn't start here, and to celebrate them all is to celebrate the multicultural nature of Australia. Just as we go to the beach rather than play in the snow on Christmas morning, enjoying a warm spring night and making a community catch-up out of Halloween lets us put our own unique spin on the occasion.

Tips

- The writer devotes considerable space at the beginning of her piece to explaining the aspects of Halloween she once objected to. Consider how this primes readers, particularly those who might also feel negatively about Halloween, to be prepared to think differently about it, as the writer herself has come to do. It also helps to present the writer as open-minded and reasonable, since she is willing to change her thinking when she finds new evidence or ideas. This is likely to encourage readers to trust that her opinion will be logical and considered.
- The two images present different perspectives on Halloween, reinforcing the argument presented in the written text, which moves from detailing one viewpoint against Halloween to endorsing a contrasting viewpoint in favour of Halloween. The first image focuses on the excesses of the celebration, with an abundance of lollies carelessly spilling out of a large bucket. Because of the image's position within the text near the writer's reference to 'mass consumption of lollies', the reader is steered towards viewing this image negatively. However, the writer goes on to admit 'sneaking a few lollies', a confession intended to present her as relatable and also signalling a shift in her argument and her opinion of Halloween. As she goes on to outline its many benefits, reinforced by the second image of smiling, costumed children, the reader is prompted to reconsider the first image as one of innocent and understandable occasional indulgence.
- The second image helps to support this reframing by presenting happy children, possibly siblings, enjoying a shared experience. One child holds a bowl of lollies while the other two hold carved pumpkins, a reminder that the day is more about shared activities such as pumpkin carving than it is about sugar consumption. The typical costumes worn by the three, together with these stereotypical Halloween props, convey the idea that this is the essence of the occasion – innocent fun and togetherness.
- Note the way in which the writer anticipates and gently rebuts a common argument against celebrating Halloween in Australia – that it is a custom imported from the United States. By acknowledging that she herself once shared this objection, reminding readers that other widely enjoyed customs are also imported, and asserting that they have the power to put their 'own unique spin' on Halloween, she encourages readers to reassess their preconceptions without compromising their belief in the importance of uniquely Australian traditions.

Scenario 8: The Salty Boot

Instructions

- In this section, you are required to analyse the use of argument(s) and language to persuade an intended audience to share the point of view expressed in an unseen persuasive text.
- Read the background information on this page and the material on the following pages, and write an analytical response to the task below.
- For the purposes of this task, the term 'language' refers to written and spoken language, and 'visuals' refers to images and graphics.
- This section is worth one-third of the total marks for the examination.

Task

Write an analysis of the ways in which argument(s), written and spoken language, and visuals are used in the material on the following pages to try to persuade the intended audience to share the point of view presented.

Background information

Iconic live-music venue The Salty Boot – colloquially known as 'the Boot' – is being forced to close down due to pressure from new local residents of the inner-city suburb of Metropolo in Melbourne. These new residents say the venue is too noisy and this has become a problem for the increasing number of people moving to the popular area. A group of musicians, music fans and longstanding local residents are campaigning against the closure. Vince D'Angelo, a local rock musician, is speaking at the campaign rally. The following is a transcript of his speech

A flyer for the rally – created by cartoonist and long-time supporter of The Salty Boot, Roisin McCrae – is included at the end of the transcript.

Ladies, gentlemen, music fans.

It's with a heavy heart that I stand before you today.

Behind me is our beloved Salty Boot, which, if those complainers get their way, will call last drinks this afternoon, and retire that old sound system.

The new gentrified[1] neighbourhood we find ourselves in has spoken, and, by their thinking, The Salty Boot no longer fits with the suburb's trendy aesthetic, or its new reputation for quiet inner-city living. This is despite the fact that a recent survey by a renowned firm has indicated that the majority of people living in Metropolo, and over 80% of Melbourne residents, want the Boot to remain open.

The Salty Boot is too loud. It's too colourful. And, most offensive of all, it's too proud of it.

From next week they'll start the process of changing this glorious building into a hairdressing salon, a furniture emporium or, more likely, a hip cafe.

And some might say, so what? A loud and filthy pub? Good riddance.

But they don't know this place like we do.

When I look at the dirty building behind us, I see much more than a filthy pub – I see a home. And I know many of you feel the same way.

This is the place where I heard live rock-and-roll for the first time, played my first ever gig on a rusted bass guitar, ordered my first beer and spent many a night in the company of good friends. It was my refuge when things were tough, and the only place I ever felt I could be who I wanted to be.

The Salty Boot, as any of you can attest, is a special place, full of life, love and, of course, great music, and it deserves to be preserved – for my sake, for yours and for this city's.

For the last 40 years, The Salty Boot has supported emerging artists. It welcomed us, and let us perform when no other entertainment venue would. Without the Boot, many of us, including myself and the internationally acclaimed musician Trombone Jackson, would not have become the famous and successful musicians we are today.

Say goodbye to the Boot, and we say goodbye to more than the building, or to chicken that tastes like tyre rubber.

Say goodbye to the Boot and we're one step closer to living in a world of cool nothingness, where band t-shirts belong on walls, where street art is commissioned for tidy sums and music is for working out to, rather than really *feeling*.

Say goodbye to the Boot and we're three-quarters of the way to boring, headed for Plainsville.

Where will people go to forget about the drudgery of everyday life, to bliss out to the sound of a soaring guitar? Where will they go to find the freedom to be themselves, to let it all hang out? And where will they go to see and hear some of the incredible musicality and creativity our city has to offer?

This wasn't on the menu at my local hipster cafe, last time I checked.

But there's also the next crop of music fans to think about. The disappearance of the Boot would be a tragedy for me, sure, but what about my kids? What about a whole generation who will never get to experience the magic of this place firsthand?

What about aspiring musicians who may never be able to advance their careers, because they have nowhere that will allow them to perform and demonstrate their potential? How many future Trombone Jacksons could remain undiscovered?

As an ageing rocker, I've seen friends change over the years: from watching gentrification in our suburbs with disgust, to leading the charge for gentrification themselves.

We had all the benefits of letting loose at The Salty Boot, but now that we're older, more delicate, our generation wants to shut it down.

Because it's too loud. Too loud!

I don't know about you, but when I was a youngster we turned it up to eleven. We drank and screamed and danced all night long, we made art and rock-and-roll – but let these kids do the same?

Absolutely not.

Those of my generation had their fun, and now they're out to ensure that the only thing approaching expression and creativity our children can appreciate is latte art[2].

Well, folks, I for one am not going to let them destroy this place.

I'm not prepared to say goodbye just yet – and I don't think you are either.

Show your support. Sign the petition to keep our Salty Boot dark, dingy and dirty – and as loud (and proud) as it wants to be. Thank you.

[1]**gentrified** – describes a previously poor neighbourhood that wealthier people have moved into, forcing original residents out and changing the character of the area
[2]**latte art** – designs in the milk foam on top of coffee drinks

Tips

- Note how the layout of the text reflects the speaker's delivery: he uses strong declamatory sentences and frequent pauses to allow his points to be easily absorbed by listeners.
- He also uses frequent rhetorical questions that encourage the listener to reflect on all that might be lost with the closure of The Salty Boot. The way in which these form a list of potential losses makes the situation seem serious and implies that much more is at stake than just a place to hear live music. These questions also lend his speech gravity and importance, inclining his audience to pay attention. Moreover, this repetitious strategy has associations with poetry and music, a reminder to the audience of the value of live performance.
- Examine the speaker's tone and the ways in which he uses humour and emotional appeals to stir both nostalgia and a sense of outrage in his audience.
- The speaker's own personality and experiences are a key element of his argument. Look for the points at which he refers to himself and consider the persona he projects and how this might incline the audience to respond to his point of view.
- Examine the visual style of the flyer and the way in which the visual tone supports the speaker's tone. Take into account the fact that the flyer's creator, like D'Angelo, is a long-time supporter of the venue, and consider how their joint purpose and shared approach is likely to strengthen their argument in the minds of the audience.

Scenario 9: Golf course development

Instructions

- In this section, you are required to analyse the use of argument(s) and language to persuade an intended audience to share the point of view expressed in an unseen persuasive text.
- Read the background information on this page and the material on the following pages, and write an analytical response to the task below.
- For the purposes of this task, the term 'language' refers to written and spoken language, and 'visuals' refers to images and graphics.
- This section is worth one-third of the total marks for the examination.

Task

Write an analysis of the ways in which argument(s), written and spoken language, and visuals are used in the material on the following pages to try to persuade the intended audience to share the point of view presented.

Background information

A new golf course development has been proposed for the old Showgrounds area in Westhaven. The local council has not yet approved the proposal. One of the landscape architects working on the project, Alejandra Ortega, addressed a community gathering to inform them about the development plans. The following is a transcript of her speech, along with two of the projected images from the presentation.

Good evening, my fellow community members, and thank you for joining me here tonight to discuss this amazing opportunity. I'm going to tell you a little bit more about our plans, and invite your feedback on ways that we can make this development even more exciting and inclusive. For those of you who don't know me, I'm Alejandra Ortega, and I am the director of Ortega Landscape Design. But far more importantly I'm a local Westhaven girl through and through. I grew up here – just round the corner on Regan Street, actually – and I love this town as much as you all clearly do. Which is why, when Goodgreens Developers approached my firm to design their new golf course, I immediately said yes.

Figures from the ausgolf website show that Australia has more golf clubs per capita than almost any other country. Did you know that, in 2020, golf participation in Australia showed the highest increase of any organised sport? An official Sport Australia survey showed that 250 000 more Australians played golf than in the previous year. Despite COVID – or perhaps even because of it – more and more Australians are beginning to enjoy the benefits of the sport. Seeking a gentle form of aerobic exercise? Golf! Looking for a like-minded community to share physical and social activity with? Golf! Hoping to improve your hand-eye coordination and develop your ability to hit a really small white ball with a really thin stick into a tiny hole a really long way away? Golf, golf, golf!

Now, I know that many of you are concerned about the proposed location for the new course, at the old Westhaven Showgrounds. Currently, as you probably all know, the grounds are managed by the council. They are freely accessible to the public and can be booked for community activities such as parties, school events and weddings. However, our research, with the support of the council, shows that public bookings for the area have declined by over 40% in the last four years. This indicates that the community is not making use of the facilities. While I know some people still come to run on the oval, take their kids to the playground and occasionally use the barbecue areas, this is not enough to justify leaving the area undeveloped.

The Showgrounds is an underutilised space that the council cannot afford to maintain properly, and it is becoming tragically run down. The rusting grandstand, dilapidated fencing and old toilet block urgently need upgrading as well as ongoing maintenance. This will require new and sustainable revenue streams. If you have a look at the photo on the screen behind me, you will see exactly what I mean.

We all want to have pride in our local environment, and building a golf course at the Showgrounds will rejuvenate this space not only for tourists but also for our own local residents. Now, have a look at this next slide. This is what our new space could look like – isn't that a terrific improvement?!

The partnership between Goodgreens Developers and Ortega Landscape Design has so much to offer our community. As private developers, we have a significant budget, meaning that we can bring the Showgrounds to life in a way that has not been seen since the days when the site hosted the bustling, exciting Westhaven Shows many decades ago. The proposed Greenhaven Golf Club will value-add to our community. It will give residents the opportunity to nurture or begin a passion for golf without having to travel away from Westhaven. It will revitalise an area that is not appreciated currently. And, perhaps most significantly, it will bring much-needed tourist dollars. We have a beautiful and vibrant town, and now is the time to showcase it to travellers.

Many of you fear losing your community space. But let me assure you that the project is not designed to alienate anyone. The development plan – which is here for you to view tonight – includes a club restaurant open to the public, a special mini-golf course dedicated to introducing children to the sport, and a purpose-built public running track that will take advantage of the new greenscape the club will generate. Far from losing a space, you will find a whole new world open to you at Greenhaven, whether you are a dedicated golfer or a health-conscious Westhaven resident seeking fresh air and exercise in beautiful, well-kept parklands.

Please feel free to come up and chat with me shortly about any questions or concerns you may have. We expect this development proposal to be approved in the next few months, and we want to be sure we have had the input of all our most valued stakeholders, both financial and personal – and that means you.

Thanks for your time, and I look forward to seeing you on the greens!

Tips

» Be aware of the speaker's vested interest in the golf course development, which she reveals at the outset of her speech ('I am the director of Ortega Landscape Design'). In declaring this upfront she aims to present herself as open and honest in order to establish trust in her audience; while this position obviously suggests a potential bias in her viewpoint, it also indicates a level of knowledge and expertise about the site and proposed development.

» Note, however, the way in which she moves quickly on from this point to emphasise her connection to the local area ('But far more importantly I'm a local Westhaven girl through and through'), thus conveying the impression that her opinion on the development derives from her knowledge and love of the place in which she grew up, rather than any business interest in the golf course.

» Ortega creates an extended appeal to civic pride in her speech, reminding her audience that they live in a 'beautiful and vibrant town' and invoking shame at the current state of the Showgrounds site through the description of it as 'run down', supported by the photograph showing the dingy and damaged stands. The contrasting second image depicts the sunlit proposed golf course; showing children using the facilities associates the golf course with the bright future Ortega describes.

» Note, too, the way in which Ortega encourages her audience to view themselves not only as 'our most valued stakeholders' but as important decision-makers. This is true of the council members who will vote on the proposed golf course, but is not the case for most of the people she addresses. Nevertheless, this flattery is intended to make her listeners feel valued and important, and thus to wish to side with the person who is evoking these positive feelings.

Scenario 10: Fast fashion

Instructions

- In this section, you are required to analyse the use of argument(s) and language to persuade an intended audience to share the point of view expressed in an unseen persuasive text.
- Read the background information on this page and the material on the following pages, and write an analytical response to the task below.
- For the purposes of this task, the term 'language' refers to written and spoken language, and 'visuals' refers to images and graphics.
- This section is worth one-third of the total marks for the examination.

Task

Write an analysis of the ways in which argument(s), written and spoken language, and visuals are used in the material on the following pages to try to persuade the intended audience to share the point of view presented.

Background information

Alessandra DuBois, owner of the second-hand clothing store Alessandra's Thrifty Chic Store, has written a lengthy post on a blog linked with her store's website. She has shared the post with followers of her store on different social media platforms.

Fast fashion? Let's slow it down

By Alessandra DuBois

Does the person in this cartoon look familiar? Someone who buys on-trend outfits and must-have accessories, without taking the time to consider the consequences of their shopping habits – in other words, a proponent of fast fashion. If this sounds like someone you know, send them this post immediately. **This is their intervention**[1].

For those of you unfamiliar with the term, 'fast fashion' refers to trendy, inexpensive clothing inspired by catwalks and/or celebrity trends and made available at rapid speed to cater to the demands of consumers. While this may sound like a good thing to those on a budget who like to keep up with trends, it ignores a toxic culture that harms the environment and exploits workers.

Currently, the fashion industry churns out 80 billion garments a year – that's 400% more than 20 years ago! And according to clothes waste charity TRAID, the average garment is only worn ten times before it is thrown away. The environmental impact of endlessly producing new clothes in this way is colossal.

Every year the fashion sector requires 93 billion cubic metres of water, and wastewater from the factories producing the clothes gets dumped directly into rivers. This toxic water, containing substances such as lead, mercury and arsenic, threatens both wildlife and humans. Furthermore, fast fashion leads to high levels of plastic pollution. Over 60% of clothes are manufactured using petrochemicals, and these fabrics are not biodegradable in nature. Also, according to the Ellen MacArthur Foundation, clothes release half a million tonnes of microfibres into the ocean every year, equivalent to more than 50 billion plastic bottles.

If that wasn't enough to scare you, the industry also has a heavy carbon footprint. *The Ethical Consumer* has suggested that the production of clothes could amount to 26% of our total carbon footprint in less than 30 years if these trends in fast fashion continue on their upward trajectory.

This highlights the urgency of the issue – it's so important that it affects the very future of our planet. You may think that something as simple as the clothes you wear on your back is insignificant – that 'this stuff … has nothing to do with you', to quote everyone's favourite fashion horror flick, *The Devil Wears Prada* – but the decisions you make today about how and where you purchase your clothes will have significant consequences for us all.

And let's not forget the human element in all of this: that is, the people who make the clothes with their own two hands, working unbearably long hours for terribly low pay (below the living wage) under extremely hazardous working conditions. Many of these workers are found in countries such as Bangladesh, China and India, where sweatshops and child labour are rife.

Given all this, how can anyone consciously continue to support fast fashion? Especially when there's such a simple fix for this issue.

As I'm sure many of you are aware, I opened Alessandra's Thrifty Chic Store two years ago. Today, it is Brunswick's premier second-hand clothing business and a great alternative to the large outlets that promote fast fashion.

Our products are all sustainably sourced and carefully selected to ensure they're made from durable materials – this means you'll get hundreds if not thousands of uses out of them before they need to be disposed of.

By encouraging our patrons to donate clothing rather than simply throwing it out, we can stop the vicious cycle of wastage, and offer people on a budget the chance to purchase stylish outfits without contributing their hard-earned dollars to an abusive system.

Second-hand clothes stores aren't the only way you can help challenge the spread of fast fashion, though. Not every fashion brand is considered fast fashion, and there is an increasing number of brands that are conscious of community and environmental issues. These are the ones who choose to use natural materials, eco-friendly manufacturing and fair labour. Purchasing garments that are made from recyclable or environmentally friendly materials, from companies such as these, will have a lower negative impact on our waterways, air and soil once you have finished using them.

Whether it's shopping at a thrift store or carefully selecting garments that you can wear for years and years, this trend of 'slow fashion' is what we need to see more of. If everyone who sees this post went to their closet right now and gathered every item of clothing they were planning to dispose of and donated them to a thrift store, we would have collectively made a sizeable difference in bringing fast fashion to a screeching halt. So, get out there and spread the message: the era of fast fashion is dead.

[1]**intervention** – an attempt by friends and/or family to confront and help a person with addiction or behavioural issues

Tips

- The writer opens with a question to the reader, with the aim of immediately capturing their attention. The directness of this approach is likely to be well received by her target audience of readers who are probably familiar with her social media profile and already interested in fashion. The description of the female figure who appears in the image at the start of the blog post aims to retain this attention through its familiarity and relatability.
- The instruction to the reader to 'send … this post immediately' to anyone they believe resembles the person DuBois describes in her opening paragraph fulfils multiple purposes. It continues the direct address and intimate tone established from the outset, which draws on the existing relationship between the writer and many of her readers to deepen rapport. It implies that her readers are likely to recognise this type of person in their own lives, suggesting the problem of fast fashion is significant. It also further promotes the writer's own social media presence and business under the guise of an 'intervention', a word usually used to describe the loving involvement of family and friends in an addict's treatment.
- Consider the two types of argument DuBois presents for rejecting fast fashion: that it is unethical, and that not buying fast fashion is easy and beneficial for consumers, as implied with phrases such as 'simple fix' and 'you'll get hundreds if not thousands of uses out of them'. In this way she positions readers to think that shopping ethically is good for the environment, for others and for themselves.

Scenario 11: Sunflower plantations

Instructions

- In this section, you are required to analyse the use of argument(s) and language to persuade an intended audience to share the point of view expressed in an unseen persuasive text.
- Read the background information on this page and the material on the following pages, and write an analytical response to the task below.
- For the purposes of this task, the term 'language' refers to written and spoken language, and 'visuals' refers to images and graphics.
- This section is worth one-third of the total marks for the examination.

Task

Write an analysis of the ways in which argument(s), written and spoken language, and visuals are used in the material on the following pages to try to persuade the intended audience to share the point of view presented.

Background information

The small town of Sunnyside is well known for its sunflower plantations, a major contributor to the town's economy. Recently, Sunnyside has been inundated with tourists visiting the fields and taking photos. The number of visitors has caused stress to the crops and is upsetting farmers. One farmer, Harvey Sunshine, called an emergency council meeting to address the problem. The following is a transcript of the speech he delivered, with a photograph that accompanied the speech.

Ladies and gentleman of our beloved community: for those who don't know, my name is Harvey Sunshine, long-time local of Sunnyside and resident curmudgeon[1].

Most of you have come to know me as the man with a constant axe to grind[2], and while that reputation is partly warranted, it's not something I take lightly: every now and then, axes need grinding and we must speak our mind, loudly and clearly.

I've called this meeting today to talk about an issue of increasing concern for our community.

For the past two summers, I, like many of my fellow farmers, have been dealing with a huge increase in the number of tourists visiting my sunflower fields.

Tourists have always been a presence at Sunnyside. We live in a beautiful part of the world, after all, and the sunflowers in full bloom are something truly special to behold.

But the sheer number arriving in the summer months is causing havoc across the region. People tell me it's a 'social media' problem, and that what these folks are after is a photo or two to share on the internet.

But the damage they're willing to cause in the service of that one perfect shot is, frankly, disturbing.

They arrive in hordes – sometimes hundreds a day – parking along the single road that runs by my property, clogging up the traffic.

They come armed to the teeth with 'selfie sticks' and snacks.

Some of them – the decent ones – enter through my front gate and ask permission to take a photo, but the rest are scaling my fence, or cutting the wires.

Harvey Sunshine inspects his sunflowers for damage.

I've seen people trample hundreds of dollars underfoot. I've seen others snap the heads off my plants and take them home. You'll see in the photo I've put up on the wall behind me the kinds of damage I'm witnessing daily in the summer.

And it's not just the plants that are suffering. My two dogs, Banjo and Lucky, are in a constant state of anxiety and hypervigilance due to the constant intrusions. My cat, Millicent, is scared to step foot outside most days, for fear of being hounded for pats and pictures by perfect strangers. And long gone are the days when I could let the grandkids wander freely among the fields – no chance of that when I've no idea who they might encounter in a place they ought to be able to have free and private enjoyment of.

That word – 'private' – is a key one. Call me old-fashioned but I think it's something we can still, even in this publicity-obsessed age, reasonably expect in our own homes and backyards.

And yet I've spent days clearing litter from my property and hours arguing with the idiots who think they have a right to wander around my farm without a care in the world.

'Well, what's to be done?' you ask.

As far as the council is concerned, there's nothing we can do. 'Put up and shut up until the season is over,' they tell us.

Absolute cowardice!

We need urgent action if sunflowers are to have any kind of future here in our community.

My solution? Simple. Or, at least, simple economics. If these people want to take photos of the crops then we should let them – but at a price. I'm suggesting we farmers charge a fee to the tourists who enter our property and take photos of the flowers.

This is, after all, a very fragile plant, and one that only blooms during a small window of time in the year.

Charging these people is a way to help our farmers get through the non-productive season with a little extra to invest when the next crop comes around.

It's not just the farmers who would benefit, either. Think of what a boon a little extra money would be to our community, to our local businesses.

And then there are the opportunities to explore new ventures. Coffee carts outside every farm. Local markets selling fresh produce from around the region. The potential is limitless.

I know of a number of towns in other regions doing the same thing. Dandyville is already reaping the benefits of asking tourists to pay to see their flower plantations, and we can't let them get ahead of us.

Whether you can believe it or not, people are willing to pay to take photos of our sunflowers, and we have a choice: let them do so, or let our farmers pay the price for leaving the situation as it is. And take it from me, we farmers won't – can't – afford to pay these costs indefinitely. I don't want to shut up shop or be forced out of the home I love. But the situation has reached a crisis point.

So I'm calling on all of you to support our farmers and get behind our community. Support my motion for implementing a town-wide price of admission to our sunflower fields. Support our local businesses. Support the future of Sunnyside!

[1]**curmudgeon** – a bad-tempered or grumpy person
[2]**axe to grind** – an issue with someone or something

Tips

- Think about why Sunshine might begin by describing himself as a ‘curmudgeon’ with an ‘axe to grind’, an unflattering characterisation. What is the likely impact of this on an audience of mostly local people and how might it prepare them to receive his opinion?
- Consider why Sunshine might have chosen to place a photo of himself in the sunflower fields behind him as he speaks. Together with his humorous description of himself, it works to suggest a gruff but good-hearted persona, whose perspective on the issue can be relied upon to be sincere. The warm light of the sunshine in the image, as well as Sunshine’s gentle inspection of the flowers, suggests his genuine care for them and supports his argument for protecting them.
- Although he describes in some detail the impact of visitors on his sunflower plantation, Sunshine also notes the impact on his animals, grandchildren, other farmers and the community generally, thus suggesting that he is as concerned for others as he is for himself and his financial interests. This impression of compassion is likely to resonate with an audience consisting of people who probably have their own land, families and animals that they want to protect.
- Look at the language Sunshine uses to describe the visitors – for example, words such as ‘hordes’, ‘clogging’, ‘strangers’ – and reflect on the overall impression he builds up of these tourists. Contrast this with the image he presents of vulnerable plants and farmers and consider how this contributes to the ‘us and them’ dynamic he aims to promote, with the heedless visitors threatening the innocent residents of Sunnyside.

Scenario 12: Video games in the English classroom

Instructions

- In this section, you are required to analyse the use of argument(s) and language to persuade an intended audience to share the point of view expressed in an unseen persuasive text.
- Read the background information on this page and the material on the following pages, and write an analytical response to the task below.
- For the purposes of this task, the term 'language' refers to written and spoken language, and 'visuals' refers to images and graphics.
- This section is worth one-third of the total marks for the examination.

Task

Write an analysis of the ways in which argument(s), written and spoken language, and visuals are used in the material on the following pages to try to persuade the intended audience to share the point of view presented.

Background information

Margaret Lee has been invited to participate in a state conference for English teachers. An experienced English teacher, she has spent the past few years developing resources to help teachers incorporate video games into their English courses. The following is a transcript of the presentation she made at the start of her workshop. Two images were projected on a screen while she was speaking, each shown at different points during her speech as indicated by their placement in the transcript.

Good afternoon to my fellow English teachers. Thank you for welcoming me to speak to you today. I'm here to present a new opportunity for your students, one that will offer them an exciting new way to learn, to analyse and to study English.

I'm talking, of course, about video games.

Now, I understand that some of you have been teaching English for decades, and might never have thought of video games as a learning tool. You might even believe that video games lead to aggression and laziness. But these past few years I've been working with schools to incorporate video games into their English courses with great success.

So I ask you to forget about the violent, repetitive games you might have encountered before, and allow me to introduce you to a new world of English texts, the modern universe of video games.

Long gone are the days of punching sticky buttons in an arcade, pointlessly trying to beat your high score. Long gone are the days of zoning out in front of the TV in a darkened room, spending hours trying to master an impossible level.

The games I'm talking about are infinitely more sophisticated. In fact, they are closer to works of art than to actual games. They include engaging storylines, stunning animation and moving music scores, much like some of the films that we're already so used to analysing in English classrooms.

Furthermore, video games have several advantages over other texts.

Most video games offer an open world for the player to explore, meaning they make their own choices as they play. These choices then have consequences later in the game, so the concept of narrative structure is embedded into the act of playing. Additionally, players are able to take on new identities as they play, allowing them to empathise with characters who are very different from themselves.

Cognitive scientists have carried out several studies that suggest playing video games can improve decision-making skills and increase coordination, things that can't be developed while merely reading a novel.

And that's just the start of it.

Some video games on the market present historically accurate worlds, which can give students an advantage as they learn about historical context. Side quests and background characters can provide insight into the conventions of a genre and how society functions within that world. From exploring a precise replica of an ancient Italian city to helping a woman with a lame horse in the Wild West, playing these games can help students retain clear visual memories of the text they're studying, much more easily than if they were reading words printed on a page.

When I was still teaching English myself – I won't lie to you – I hated the idea of replacing even one of the texts on my list with a video game. I couldn't imagine removing any novel, play or group of poems. For some of my students, those books were likely to be the only classics they would ever have the opportunity to study. And how many of us would choose to play a game with killer robots when we could curl up with a book by our favourite author?

Then I considered my students.

I considered what makes them excited to learn.

I considered the world outside my classroom.

I considered the challenges that some of my students face with English.

And I knew I needed to put aside my own preferences in order to help them. For some, the English class is the worst part of their day. We forget how difficult it can be to relate to characters and situations from hundreds of years ago. For some, the task of finishing a class novel can be arduous, and it can even discourage struggling students from reading outside of class.

Video games give them a chance to really engage with a text in a more relaxed and fun way, while still learning how to analyse and interpret. Once they learn those tools, don't you think those students will feel a bit more confident about picking up that novel again?

Of course, I understand that some of you are feeling reluctant to take this big step in your classrooms. After all, we're English teachers! We wouldn't be here if we didn't love the written word. But we can't deny that video games are becoming more and more advanced.

It would be a shame to leave these rich texts unexplored when we have them right at our fingertips.

Tips

- Notice the way in which Lee repeatedly references her own experiences as a teacher to establish her credentials with her audience of fellow teachers. This is aimed at helping them feel that she understands the challenges of the classroom as well as their potential reluctance to use video games as texts, a reluctance she admits to having once shared. In this way she encourages them to share her journey from scepticism to appreciation.
- This appeal to her audience as fellow professional educators is extended through her references to terminology associated with English teaching, such as 'genre', 'narrative structure' and 'rich texts'. The use of this familiar language is intended to reassure teachers that Lee is experienced and knowledgeable, and that therefore her conclusions are likely to be reliable.
- Reflecting the fact that this is a spoken text, several sentences are set as standalone paragraphs, around which Lee would allow brief pauses. This technique highlights key points and allows the audience time to absorb them.
- The repeated 'I considered' standalone statements serve multiple functions: they remind the listener that Lee's position has been arrived at after careful contemplation; they encourage listeners to themselves take time to consider new perspectives on video games, just as Lee has; they emphasise that students' needs should be prioritised in the context of this debate; and they lend Lee's claims gravity and a sense of significance.

Scenario 13: Keeping cats indoors

Instructions

- In this section, you are required to analyse the use of argument(s) and language to persuade an intended audience to share the point of view expressed in an unseen persuasive text.
- Read the background information on this page and the material on the following pages, and write an analytical response to the task below.
- For the purposes of this task, the term 'language' refers to written and spoken language, and 'visuals' refers to images and graphics.
- This section is worth one-third of the total marks for the examination.

Task

Write an analysis of the ways in which argument(s), written and spoken language, and visuals are used in the material on the following pages to try to persuade the intended audience to share the point of view presented.

Background information

The following article, by a team of professors and academics about the danger outdoor cats can pose to local wildlife, was first published on *The Conversation*.

One cat, one year, 110 native animals: lock up your pet, it's a killing machine

By Jaana Dielenberg, Brett Murphy, Chris Dickman, John Woinarski, Leigh-Ann Woolley, Mike Calver and Sarah Legge

We know feral cats are an enormous problem for wildlife – across Australia, feral cats collectively kill more than three billion animals per year. Cats have played a leading role in most of Australia's 34 mammal extinctions since 1788, and are a big reason populations of at least 123 other threatened native species are dropping.

But pet cats are wreaking havoc too. Our analysis compiles the results of 66 different studies to gauge the impact of Australia's pet cat population on the country's wildlife.

The results are staggering. On average, each roaming pet cat kills 186 reptiles, birds and mammals per year, most of them native to Australia. Collectively, that's 4,440 to 8,100 animals per square kilometre per year for the area inhabited by pet cats.

If you own a cat and want to protect wildlife, you should keep it inside. In Australia, 1.1 million pet cats are contained 24 hours a day by responsible pet owners. The remaining 2.7 million pet cats – 71% of all pet cats – are able to roam and hunt. What's more, your pet cat could be getting out without you knowing. A radio tracking study in Adelaide found that of the 177 cats whom owners believed were inside at night, 69 cats (39%) were sneaking out for nocturnal adventures.

Surely not my cat

Just over one-quarter of Australian households (27%) have pet cats, and about half of cat-owning households have two or more cats. Many owners believe their animals don't hunt because they never come across evidence of killed animals.

But studies that used cat video tracking collars or scat analysis (checking what's in the cat's poo) have established many pet cats kill animals without bringing them home. On average, pet cats bring home only 15% of their prey.

Collectively, roaming pet cats kill 390 million animals per year in Australia.

This huge number may lead some pet owners to think their own cat's contribution wouldn't make much difference. However, we found even single pet cats have driven declines and complete losses of populations of some native animal species in their area. Documented cases have included: a feather-tailed glider population in south-eastern NSW; a skink population in a Perth suburb; and an olive legless lizard population in Canberra.

Urban cats

On average, an individual feral cat in the bush kills 748 reptiles, birds and mammals a year – four times the toll of a hunting pet cat. But feral cats and pet cats roam over very different areas. Pet cats are confined to cities and towns, where you'll find 40 to 70 roaming cats per square kilometre. In the bush there's only one feral cat for every three to four square kilometres. So while each pet cat kills fewer animals than a feral cat, their high urban density means the toll is still very high. Per square kilometre per year, pet cats kill 30–50 times more animals than feral cats in the bush.

Most of us want to see native wildlife around towns and cities. But such a vision is being compromised by this extraordinary level of predation, especially as the human population grows and our cities expand.

Pet cats living near areas with nature also hunt more, reducing the value of places that should be safe havens for wildlife. The 186 animals each pet cat kills per year on average is made up of 110 native animals (40 reptiles, 38 birds and 32 mammals). For example, the critically endangered western ringtail possum is found in suburban areas of Mandurah, Bunbury, Busselton and Albany. The possum did not move into these areas – rather, we moved into their habitat.

What can pet owners do?

Keeping your cat securely contained 24 hours a day is the only way to prevent it from killing wildlife.

It's a myth that a good diet or feeding a cat more meat will prevent hunting: even cats that aren't hungry will hunt. Various devices, such as bells on collars, are commercially marketed with the promise of preventing hunting. While some of these items may reduce the rate of successful kills, they don't prevent hunting altogether.

And they don't prevent cats from disturbing wildlife. When cats prowl and hunt in an area, wildlife have to spend more time hiding or escaping. This reduces the time spent feeding themselves or their young, or resting. In Mandurah, WA, the disturbance and hunting of just one pet cat and one stray cat caused the total breeding failure of a colony of more than 100 pairs of fairy terns.

Benefits of a life indoors

Keeping cats indoors protects pet cats from injury, avoids nuisance behaviour and prevents unwanted breeding. Cats allowed outside often get into fights with other cats, even when they're not the fighting type (they can be attacked by other cats).

Roaming cats are also very prone to getting hit by vehicles. According to the Humane Society of the United States, indoor cats live up to four times longer than those allowed to roam freely.

Indoor cats have lower rates of cat-borne diseases, some of which can infect humans. For example, in humans the cat-borne disease toxoplasmosis can cause illness, miscarriages and birth defects.

But Australia is in a very good position to make change. Compared to many other countries, the Australian public are more aware of how cats threaten native wildlife and more supportive of actions to reduce those impacts.

It won't be easy. But since more than one million pet cats are already being contained, reducing the impacts from pet cats is clearly possible if we take responsibility for them.

Tips

- The image at the beginning of the piece neatly encapsulates the issue from the outset, vividly supporting the writers' argument about cats' potential for destruction. The fact that the cat depicted is an average-sized common domestic cat encourages readers to recognise that their own pets could be part of the problem, while the dead or injured bird is a stark reminder of the damage cats can do to smaller, innocent creatures. The cat also looms over the bird, taking up most of the image's frame, highlighting the danger it presents to local wildlife.
- This text relies heavily on facts and statistics, which is linked to its place of publication – on the website of *The Conversation*, which publishes pieces by journalists and academics based on rigorous research. This context of publication means that the reader expects a certain level of fact-checking and logical rigour, thus inclining them to place more trust in the writers' conclusions.
- This reliance on research is supported by the writers' straightforward and definite tone. They make many declarative statements – for example, 'we know feral cats are an enormous problem for wildlife' and 'if you own a cat and want to protect wildlife, you should keep it inside'. Such statements leave little room for disagreement, conveying the impression that the writers are presenting indisputable facts and positioning the reader to accept their views as authoritative.
- Understanding that many of their readers will be cat-owners themselves, the writers are careful to emphasise the benefits of keeping cats indoors in terms of cat welfare. Ending with this point of argument aims to leave the reader with a positive impression of the practice of keeping cats inside, rather than a sense that the animals will be disadvantaged by an indoor existence.

Scenario 14: Tax on red meat

Instructions

- In this section, you are required to analyse the use of argument(s) and language to persuade an intended audience to share the point of view expressed in an unseen persuasive text.
- Read the background information on this page and the material on the following pages, and write an analytical response to the task below.
- For the purposes of this task, the term 'language' refers to written and spoken language, and 'visuals' refers to images and graphics.
- This section is worth one-third of the total marks for the examination.

Task

Write an analysis of the ways in which argument(s), written and spoken language, and visuals are used in the material on the following pages to try to persuade the intended audience to share the point of view presented.

Background information

Parminder Preciosa is a columnist for a local newspaper. Her opinion piece calling for a tax on red meat appears on the following pages.

Taxing the T-bone: it's time to give red meat the chop

By Parminder Preciosa

Allow me to set the scene.

It's lunchtime at your favourite al fresco restaurant and you've just placed your order. One glass of wine and the special of the day, your favourite: sausages and mash.

The food arrives promptly and the waiter departs with a top-up of your glass and a kindly 'bon appétit'.

The moment you've been waiting for is here, but just as you ready yourself to take that first bite – fork in hand, napkin in collar, salivating at the expectation – you smell it.

Smoke.

Cigarette smoke, specifically.

Wafting over to your table. Stinging your eyes. Clinging to the insides of your nostrils.

The culprit is well within the legal range from your seat (you've checked), but it doesn't matter – the odour is overpowering. Your potatoes with thyme have taken on a horrible taste; your glass of red wine resembles a puddle on a dirty road.

It's disgusting, you think to yourself. Another selfish smoker, poisoning themselves – and those in the wider radius – with their dirty vice, taking up your tax dollars and making life uncomfortable for everyone else.

You're mad. You're furious. You're going to say something! And, to be honest, not many people would blame you.

Because, there's no doubt, it's easy to get angry about smoking in the twenty-first century.

The latest statistics suggest that 10.6 per cent of Australia's adults smoke, and the government is making sure those who can't quit know all about the cost of their habit, both to our society and to themselves.

Cigarettes are now taxed to high heaven, and the packages they come in are covered in images of the gruesome medical conditions that can befall even the most casual puffer.

But while you might be hyper-aware of the dangers of smoking, there's another killer in this picture, and it's hiding in plain sight. Yep, right there, next to your mash.

I'm talking about the sausages. Red meat: delicious, maybe, but just as much of a threat to your health as that packet of cigs.

The World Health Organization (WHO) now classifies red meat as a carcinogen[1], with the consumption of processed varieties showing an elevated risk to humans.

According to *BMJ Global Health Journal*, if people were to replace their red meat with small fish such as sardines, herring and anchovies, up to 750 000 premature deaths from non-communicable diseases such as stroke or colon cancer could be prevented by 2050, especially in low- and middle-income countries. A study published in *Proceedings of the National Academy of Sciences* found that up to 16 000 deaths in the United States can be attributed to air pollution caused by food production, and 80 per cent of these are the result of animal-related food production, including meat production.

But mention any of these statistics to the average person, and you're sure to draw looks of incredulity.

Pepperoni pizza, bacon and eggs – fatal? But they're so delicious!

Sorry, people, but that's pretty much what they said about cigarettes once upon a time.

It wasn't easy to change the way we as a society think about smoking, and it's not going to be easy to change the way we think about red meat, either.

But just because something is difficult in the beginning, that doesn't mean it isn't worth doing.

It's time to treat meat the way we treat other threats to human health, and the first step should be taxing consumption.

Taxes such as the ones we have on cigarettes would address the enormous strain on our health budgets associated with eating red meat.

Taxes would also have positive knock-on effects that go beyond the economic, like encouraging people to make healthier choices.

But even if the health argument won't convince you, there are many other reasons for bringing in a meat tax.

One issue worth considering is how red meat production is affecting the planet.

Livestock farming is posing a catastrophic risk to our ecosystem, from the large amounts of greenhouse gases animals produce and the water needed to sustain them (500 grams of beef is estimated to require some 7000 litres of water), to the acres of carbon-absorbing forests being cleared to accommodate more farms. And with demand for red meat growing globally, the problem is only going to get worse.

Animal rights groups have also pointed to the sometimes appalling ways we treat the animals we eat, including the unethical practices adopted to raise and slaughter millions of cows and pigs each year. (Australia kills an astonishing 170 000 cattle alone each week.)

The case, then – to my mind, at least – is clear. And in some ways it's more persuasive than the arguments for taxing cigarettes.

Red meat has costs: economically, ethically and in terms of our health. And while it's nobody's right to dictate what people can and can't do, it's reasonable that individuals should pay for those activities that place a burden on all of us, be it smoking that cigarette or tucking into a steak.

[1]**carcinogen** – a substance that can increase the risk of cancer

Tips

» Preciosa opens with an extended description of a diner being disturbed by cigarette smoke. The details she includes to paint the picture – such as the meal ordered and the waiter's words – together with the distinctive use of the second-person 'you', invite readers to place themselves in this situation and encourage them to feel the same disgust and upset provoked by the fictional smoker. This suggests to readers that the dislike of cigarette smoke is universal, thus preparing them for her main argument that they should feel similarly about meat.

» The comparison between the familiar and widely accepted opinion that cigarette smoking is bad for one's health and the argument that meat consumption is harmful prepares the reader to accept that meat is as dangerous as smoking. Through this comparison, Preciosa associates the harm caused by cigarettes with that caused by meat, creating a connection in readers' minds that is likely to position them to want to stop eating meat or at least to reduce their meat consumption.

» In comparing meat to cigarettes, the writer aims to evoke both fear and disgust in the reader, a tactic she continues throughout her piece. The image supports this strategy by presenting a slab of raw meat on a plate, an unappetising sight that is likely to arouse the viewer's sense of disgust. The question-mark shape alludes to the dilemma of whether or not to eat red and processed meat, encouraging viewers to reflect on their choices after reading the information shared by Preciosa.

» Note that the main argument Preciosa presents is that red and processed meats are bad for people's health. She devotes the most space to this argument, presenting various forms of evidence. However, she also presents additional supporting reasons, referring to the environmental and animal welfare benefits of a meat tax. It is worth spending more time in your analysis on the way in which Preciosa unpacks and supports her primary reason than on the supplementary reasons she offers.

Scenario 15: Coffee pods

Instructions

- In this section, you are required to analyse the use of argument(s) and language to persuade an intended audience to share the point of view expressed in an unseen persuasive text.
- Read the background information on this page and the material on the following pages, and write an analytical response to the task below.
- For the purposes of this task, the term 'language' refers to written and spoken language, and 'visuals' refers to images and graphics.
- This section is worth one-third of the total marks for the examination.

Task

Write an analysis of the ways in which argument(s), written and spoken language, and visuals are used in the material on the following pages to try to persuade the intended audience to share the point of view presented.

Background information

The following opinion piece appeared on *The Conversation* website, which claims to provide 'an independent source of news and views, sourced from the academic and research community and delivered direct to the public'.

What our love affair with coffee pods reveals about our values

By John Rice and Nigel Martin

Disclosure statement

John Rice is a member of the Australian Labor Party and the National Tertiary Education Union. He drinks skinny flat whites.

Nigel Martin does not work for, consult, own shares in or receive funding from any company or organisation that would benefit from this article, and has disclosed no relevant affiliations beyond their academic appointment.

A quick shot, but then what? While some used coffee pods like these are recycled, many more end up in the bin.

Mornings just aren't the same. Late sleepers, once troubled only by the quiet gurgle of the boiling kettle, are now shaken from their slumber by the sounds of steaming water being forced through aluminium or plastic coffee pods.

The pods are conveniently secreted into the coffee machine's collecting receptacle, so the pangs of guilt from the latte socialists[1] (and others) are only tweaked when the dank pods require emptying – generally well after the coffee has been consumed.

Wooed by no less than Hollywood star George Clooney, Australia is in love with coffee pods. Pods have taken Australian homes and workplaces by storm.

As is the case for other beverages, Australians have shifted to drinking better quality coffee and pods are part of that mix. While pods are one of the most expensive ways to buy packaged coffee, they are also one of the most convenient.

The Swiss coffee pod innovators at Nespresso (a division of the food behemoth Nestlé) have been joined by usurpers including Germany's Aldi and Italy's Cafitally. Proving that patents are easier to take out than protect, Nespresso's share of the world pod market has been in steep decline. This having been said, the industry is in a rapid phase of growth – sales are soaring – and thus few are complaining.

Yet the news is not all good. Pods are emblematic of a wider problem in our society, where we often say one thing and generally do another. In this case, where many of us like to speak about being 'green' or living sustainably, even while sipping from a cup of coffee produced by an industry that is about as sustainable as an ageing Soviet nuclear power plant.

If, as some predict, pod use doubles over the next five years, an environmental tsunami is in store. In theory, pods are recyclable. But in practice they are rarely recycled, particularly the plastic variety beloved by the budget-conscious.

Instead, they end in landfill: perhaps a poignant sign for garbage archaeologists a thousand years from now of this generation's environmental profligacy.

Independent consumer group Choice reported that Nespresso had sold an estimated 28 billion capsules worldwide in a year – about 28 million kilograms of aluminium, much of which may be sitting in landfill, with recycling figures not made public.

New Zealand's Ethical Coffee Company has created a vegetable-based biodegradable coffee capsule that is Nespresso-compatible and can be thrown straight into the compost. However, the shelf life of these pods is likely to be far more limited than the most commonly used aluminium or double-wrapped plastic pods.

Environmental problems are not the only vices embodied in pods. The coffee industry has long been criticised for its sourcing practices, especially in the third world.

The Swiss multinational[2] Nestlé, which first dreamed up the pod phenomenon, is no stranger to such criticism. It runs its own 'sustainability' accreditation program, which it proudly pronounces now exceeds 75% for beans sourced. However, cynics might see the self-accreditation program as essentially self-serving, delivering few benefits or value-adding opportunities to coffee-growing communities.

Perhaps most prosaically, critics often argue that pod coffee just isn't any good.

A decent barista generally uses between 10 and 20 grams of ground coffee in a serve, while pods contain barely 5 grams. The decision to make the pods so small was carefully chosen to maximise profits, not taste.

As a result, the coffee produced generally fails blind taste tests – labelled watery, musty and underwhelming by Choice. Hardly the words that the marketers would like to hear.

And yet, the march of the pods continues.

The American satirist HL Mencken famously quipped that 'no one in this world … has ever lost money by underestimating the intelligence of the great masses of the plain people'. In today's world, you could add the word 'laziness' or, more charitably, 'love of convenience'.

Pods, in their own humble way, tell us much about the future intersection of environmentalism and consumerism.

Western consumers are generally supportive of the environment – so long as they don't have to do anything about it. Multinationals everywhere are wise to this, of course, and have created a phenomenon known to cynical greenies and academics as 'greenwashing'. This entails wrapping a product in a veil of environmentally positive haze, regardless of how fundamentally egregious its environmental credentials are.

It all paints a less than rosy picture for the future, in which more businesses help create, rather than solve, environmental problems. How this all plays out remains to be seen. One thing, however, is predictable. For innovators who can blend branding and convenience while ignoring all else, the future seems assured.

[1]**latte socialist** – a privileged person who lives in the city and has left wing views
[2]**multinational** – a type of corporation that operates in multiple countries

Tips

- The writers' overall approach, indicated in the headline, is to frame coffee pod use as part of a broader issue – that people will often act in ways contrary to their expressed values. Readers are encouraged to confront their own hypocrisy or the ways in which they might fall short of their professed environmental ideals, thus positioning them to want to behave differently in order to ease their sense of guilt.
- Analyse key words that have been carefully chosen for their particular associations. For example, the word 'tsunami', with its connotations of large-sale disaster, death and destruction, aims to evoke alarm in the reader.
- The writers are openly critical not only of coffee pod producers, whom they portray as self-interested profit-seekers, but also of consumers of coffee pods, a group that many readers might fall into. They accuse consumers of valuing 'laziness' and 'love of convenience' over the environment, and their argument is encapsulated in both the headline and the statement that 'Western consumers are generally supportive of the environment – so long as they don't have to do anything about it'. This overt criticism is intended to invoke guilt and shame in readers, if they themselves use coffee pods, and alarm and outrage in non-pod-using readers.
- The bleak conclusion, with its reference to a 'less than rosy' future, conveys the writers' pessimism about the capacity of consumers to change their behaviour, which might evoke in some readers the desire to meet the implicit challenge the writers set: to change their behaviour to match their stated environmental values.

Scenario 16: Children and screen time

Instructions

- In this section, you are required to analyse the use of argument(s) and language to persuade an intended audience to share the point of view expressed in an unseen persuasive text.
- Read the background information on this page and the material on the following pages, and write an analytical response to the task below.
- For the purposes of this task, the term 'language' refers to written and spoken language, and 'visuals' refers to images and graphics.
- This section is worth one-third of the total marks for the examination.

Task

Write an analysis of the ways in which argument(s), written and spoken language, and visuals are used in the material on the following pages to try to persuade the intended audience to share the point of view presented.

Background information

The following letter was written to the Wattletree Primary School community by a parent, Asif Abdul, the father of two students. The letter appeared in the school's weekly newsletter under the heading 'What Steve Jobs taught me about parenting'.

What Steve Jobs taught me about parenting

Dear Wattletree parents,

I've been thinking about something lately, and I'm writing this open letter to encourage you all to do the same. I've been thinking about the amount of time our children spend in front of screens.

Last week, as I was waiting at school to pick up my boys, Joshua and Braiden, I read an interesting article on my phone. It was about how Apple founder Steve Jobs limited his children's screen time.

This got me thinking. If Steve Jobs, technological guru, limited his kids' use of screens, why don't I monitor my children's use?

I did some research and discovered it wasn't only Jobs who felt this way. Several CEOs of tech companies had similar ideas.

I've often used screens to keep my kids quiet. Last week my youngest, Oliver, was with me in a cafe. It had been one of *those* mornings; I couldn't get him to settle down. I asked if he wanted to watch a video. He nodded, raising his eyes hopefully. I propped the phone against the salt shaker and pressed play. He was mesmerised. I finally had a minute to enjoy a coffee.

Later, Oliver watched an hour of television. Then he played on the computer. When his brothers came home, he watched them play video games. After dinner he watched more TV, and in bed we read an ebook on the iPad. Then, while his brothers brushed their teeth, I left the iPad beside him, playing sleep-time music. (It doubles as a night-light.)

Why am I explaining this? Because I've been thinking about the degree to which we're reliant, as parents, on technology: not only for its ability to expose children to new things, or provide answers to curly questions ('Why don't you Google it?' I always tell Braiden), but also as a substitute babysitter. I realised that for me, and I think for many others, communication devices have become an integral part of parenting. When I calculated the amount of time four-year-old Oliver spent in front of a screen, it was almost six hours per day. What effect was that having on his development?

Television, tablets, phones, computers: all these devices are used, often daily, by kids. As I read further, I found that many reputable figures are concerned by this.

The wonderful book *The Shallows* by Nicholas Carr argues that the internet is changing people's brains in insidious ways we're only beginning to understand. While books encourage a sustained level of concentration and immersion in a story-world, the internet, with its endless links, encourages a shallow, superficial engagement with information – there is always something else to click on. I see this with Braiden, who researches a school project as if running a timed obstacle course – each site only gets a glance before he clicks on something else. He's learning, yes, but what of his learning quality? Is he reflecting on, questioning, considering what he reads? Or, with so much at his fingertips, is it encouraging him to copy and repeat things, to give little thought to what he is reading?

Many doctors are worried about the effect screen time has on children's brains. Neuroscientist Susan Greenfield thinks neural pathways will change in children who spend hours a day with screens. Professor Gary Small from the US agrees. The American Academy of Pediatrics states that computers should be avoided until a child is two because 'a child's brain develops rapidly during these first years' and 'children learn best by interacting with people, not screens'.

Between computers, tablets, smart phones and television, many Australian children spend hours looking at screens every day.

There are also health problems that result from kids being constantly glued to screens. Children are less likely to spend time playing sport or exercising. Since the rise of digital technology, childhood obesity in Australia has increased at a startling rate. (Did you know that, in the decade to 1995, the number of overweight children aged 7–15 almost doubled, and the number of obese children more than tripled?) There's eye strain – on developing eyeballs – and dehydration and sleep problems (exposure to backlit screens at night can affect sleep patterns).

Cyberbullying and exposure to adult content are also risks. It's estimated that 30 per cent of Aussie children have seen something online that 'upset or bothered them'. As a parent, I try to monitor my kids' internet use, but I can't be watching every second – just as a teacher with a class full of kids can't – to ensure my son doesn't click on a bad link, or Google a 'naughty' word when my back is turned.

Some may ask: if a phone keeps your kid quiet, why worry? Well, like most parents, I want my children to become informed, creative and imaginative adults who contribute to the world in positive, meaningful ways. I have been irresponsible in my quick-fix habits: in seeing screens as a necessity, I have encouraged my children to do so too. Rather than teaching them that devices are a learning tool, I've let my kids use screens to ward off boredom or fatigue or anger. If I'm honest, I've been guilty of the belief that anything involving a screen is good, when in fact overuse might be changing my children's brains – hampering their capacity for critical thought or opening them up to a host of problems later in life. If this sounds anything like you, I hope you can learn from my mistakes.

Technology has many benefits, but Jobs was onto something. I've implemented a policy in our house: 90 minutes' screen time a day. And if I want Oliver to be quiet, I pull out crayons and ask him to draw, rather than plonk him down in front of a screen. Every night this week we've been reading print books, so he can have dreams sparked by creativity and imagination and wonder, not by blinking lights and flashing figures.

I encourage all parents to think about their children's screen use. As the saying goes, 'The medium is the message.' The way our children approach the world is being shaped by time spent with screens, and we need to be aware of the responsibilities of that.

Asif Abdul (parent)

Tips

» The headline makes use of the highly recognisable name of Steve Jobs to promote engagement with the article. Jobs was associated with the field of technology, thus the unlikely pairing of his name with the word 'parenting' is aimed at intriguing readers and enticing them to want to find out the connection between the two.

» Notice the way in which Abdul develops a confessional tone, admitting to being 'irresponsible' and to having made 'mistakes'. This helps readers to view him as both relatable and also a figure of sympathy, inclining them to trust that his opinion is both sincere and derived from experience and trial and error.

» This confessional tone is augmented by Abdul's frequent references to his own life and parenting experiences. He introduces his children to readers by name and relates personal information about their moods and habits. This helps to build the impression that he is talking confidentially, parent to parent, and imparting lessons from his own life and recent reading. This low-pressure manner of conveying his opinion could incline the reader to be more receptive to Abdul's message.

» Consider how the photograph supports Abdul's argument. The image features a child fixated on a phone, ignoring the shelves of books in the background. This, in conjunction with the caption stating that 'Australian children spend hours looking at screens every day', encourages readers to worry that phones are taking up time during which children should be engaging in other, more valuable activities, such as books. The position of the image, placed near a list of health issues caused by screens and a reference to the risks of 'cyberbullying and exposure to adult content', invites readers to consider the potential damage being caused to this child and Australian children in general due to the overwhelming amount of time they spend on screens.

Scenario 17: Overtourism

Instructions

- In this section, you are required to analyse the use of argument(s) and language to persuade an intended audience to share the point of view expressed in an unseen persuasive text.
- Read the background information on this page and the material on the following pages, and write an analytical response to the task below.
- For the purposes of this task, the term 'language' refers to written and spoken language, and 'visuals' refers to images and graphics.
- This section is worth one-third of the total marks for the examination.

Task

Write an analysis of the ways in which argument(s), written and spoken language, and visuals are used in the material on the following pages to try to persuade the intended audience to share the point of view presented.

Background information

The following article was written by journalist and travel editor Fiona Carruthers. She is senior feature writer for the *Australian Financial Review* magazine. This article was published in the Work and Careers section of that newspaper.

Overtourism: why you're the one to blame

By Fiona Carruthers

Last month, I was hiking through the wilds of Tasmania's Three Capes Track with a bunch of well-travelled people when we got talking about one of the ultimate first-world problems: overtourism. Would any of us go to Barcelona, Paris or Venice ever again? 'Heavens no,' we cried into our rye three-seed crackers. (OK, maybe to Rome in the dead of winter, or Lisbon in late spring.)

Congratulating ourselves on resisting the trend – we were in remote Tasmania, after all – we opened another bottle of white wine.

Just out of interest, I Googled a couple of figures from the vantage point of my solitary dolomite rock with its glorious ocean views and there it was: 1.3 million tourists a year into Tassie, for 519 200 locals. Uh-oh. Suddenly, we weren't talking about the problem, we were the problem. Right there, in our Patagonia fleeces with our keep cups, cheese, crackers and spicy Mexican dip, weren't we also just cluttering up the landscape?

Tourist creep: it happens so fast, we gasped. One minute you're not looking, the next minute people are climbing all over your harbour bridge, foreigners and locals alike. At least we can charge them $168 each for the privilege. Such a consolation – especially for the owners of Bridge Climb.

And yet this is one boat we're all in together. Whether you have a selfie stick or not, it gets you thinking: exactly who among us should agree not to travel? Bags not[1] putting my hand up first.

Slowing the tide

A number of ideas are circulating as to how to slow the tourist tide, one of the latest being a report from the United Nations World Tourism Organisation (UNWTO) to help cities manage the impact of tourism.

Launched at the seventh UNWTO Global Summit on Urban Tourism held in Seoul, the report fleshes out the 'complex issue' of overtourism and argues that solutions, particularly in major cities, must be forged by residents and tourists – a good point when you consider that most of us fit both descriptions at some point.

We also like to blame social media, the gig economy[2] and low-cost travel providers for this whole less-than-postcard-perfect mess. But isn't it inherent in human nature to wander, pose, paint and photograph, then return home with the victor's spoils? (Even if it is a fake Louis Vuitton leather coin purse.)

Before Facebook, even cavemen grunted about the better views from the caves down the road.

Nor do we learn our lesson. The ancient Greek travel writer Pausanias refers to Athens' crowds, and in the 1270s, Marco Polo had to navigate traders, travellers and bandits on the often busy Silk Road. By 1908, the concept of the annoying tourist was so apparent, British writer E.M. Forster wrote a novel around the theme in *A Room with a View*.

Forster writes of Florence residents pitying 'the poor tourists not a little – handed about like a parcel of goods from Venice to Florence, from Florence to Rome, living herded together in pensions or hotels, quite unconscious of anything that is outside Baedeker [travel guides], their one anxiety to get "done" or "through" and go on somewhere else'.

Sound familiar? A paper by think tank Tourism Recreation Research groans that mass tourism 'is not a new phenomenon but a process that has characterised human behaviour for many centuries'.

The only real difference is that discount airlines have made it cheaper to get there.

Whether we do it for social media or noble self-improvement is irrelevant; it seems we are hardwired to hunt down fine Egyptian cotton sheets and overpriced food, preferably with a view of the Mediterranean.

In Australia, even the tyranny of distance is no longer. It's just that no one can quite decide if that's a good or a bad thing. We all need to rethink the concept of why and how we travel – and especially how frequently.

Appeal of the staycation[3]

As a colleague who has lived abroad and speaks fluent Russian and Japanese recommended to me the other day, the staycation has rarely looked so appealing. 'You know,' he said, 'I watch all these people flying around the place – to Nepal, to the Andes and other exotic destinations – and I think, why don't you stay home? Go for a bushwalk or to the beach?'

I nodded agreement. But walking back to my desk, I suddenly wanted to ask exactly which beach, bushwalk or secret pathway he knew about, because that's what us humans do – we get ourselves in the know, be it the NSW south coast, Saint-Malo or Siberia.

Finally, for all those like me who (I'm horrified to admit) publicly lament overtourism while quietly trying to get in ahead of the pack, this was the most useful link I found while researching this column: '15 Cool Places you might not know exist in Australia'.

Lake Hillier, brace yourself. I'm coming for you next.

[1]**bags not** – said when someone wants to avoid doing something
[2]**gig economy** – an economy that relies on part-time contract workers rather than full-time employees
[3]**staycation** – a holiday near home (from stay home + vacation)

Tips

» Consider the publication in which this piece appeared, as well as the specific section – the Work and Careers section – in which it was included. What might be the characteristics of the typical reader of this section of this particular publication and how might this affect the way in which they respond to Carruthers' argument?

» Carruthers' tone is humorous and self-deprecating, as she acknowledges that she and her friends, despite their criticisms of overtourism, are also guilty of 'cluttering up the landscape'. Her description of their clothing and food draws on a popular stereotype of socially aware middle-class travellers; this ability to poke fun at herself and to recognise her own hypocrisy is intended to position readers to feel that Carruthers is both honest and down-to-earth, inclining them to trust her.

» The piece uses a problem–solution structure, outlining the nature of the issue before proposing the solution: the staycation. The use of subheadings helps the busy reader to understand this approach easily and to locate key points.

» Throughout the piece, inclusive language and references to broadly familiar experiences (such as buying a fake designer purse when on holiday) work together to characterise overtourism as a shared problem for which readers bear responsibility just as the writer admits she does. In the paragraph detailing historical complaints of overtourism, Carruthers extends this idea to present overtourism as a problem of humankind itself, asserting that it is something 'we are hardwired' for. The overall intended effect is to avoid blaming readers, but also to encourage them to feel some guilt and to recognise the issues caused by overtourism, and therefore to feel as though they should do their part to fix the problem by taking Carruthers' advice.

Scenario 18: Mobile phones and jaywalking

Instructions

- In this section, you are required to analyse the use of argument(s) and language to persuade an intended audience to share the point of view expressed in an unseen persuasive text.
- Read the background information on this page and the material on the following pages, and write an analytical response to the task below.
- For the purposes of this task, the term 'language' refers to written and spoken language, and 'visuals' refers to images and graphics.
- This section is worth one-third of the total marks for the examination.

Task

Write an analysis of the ways in which argument(s), written and spoken language, and visuals are used in the material on the following pages to try to persuade the intended audience to share the point of view presented.

Background information

The following article, published in the *Sydney Morning Herald*, was written by Wendy Squires. She is a freelance journalist, author and media consultant.

The jaywalking phone zombie plague is completely out of control

By Wendy Squires

Talk about an easy ten dollars. It was practically in my pocket already when I spotted a young guy with headphones in and phone in hand, walking along the street towards an intersection while I was driving with a friend. 'Ten bucks he won't look or even slow down before he crosses,' I challenged my mate, a man who prides himself on being far less cynical than I.

Gullibly, he took the wager. As if on cue, the bloke on the street stepped down from the footpath onto the road without breaking his stride or looking up from his phone. And while I was happy with money for nothing, a large part of me wished I had lost the bet.

Because adding to my belief that I am now officially a cranky old woman is my obsession of late with oblivious pedestrians – especially those transfixed on their phones, in my mind yet another example of the self-obsessed and entitled today who do not care about anything other than their immediate gratification, happily ignorant of spatial awareness. Forget the rest of us and our needs and rights. We simply do not exist.

Before mobile phones infiltrated society and dictated our lives, the annoying behaviour of pedestrians not paying attention to road rules was known as jaywalking and it remains the legal term for the offence today. (Before cars dominated our roads, pedestrians would refer to bad motorists as jay drivers.) The label is generally related back to the chatty jay bird in North America, and in the last century became a slang term for a stupid, gullible, ignorant, or provincial person. New York locals began calling tourists to their town jaywalkers, as they would often roam into the middle of the road to look at skyscrapers.

Today, however, there are other terms for pedestrians who flout our road rules, many unpublishable (well, the ones I've made up are, anyway). The accepted name for those who use their phones while walking today is wexter (walker and texter), and in Australia, studies show this to be as many as one in three pedestrians.

It is this distraction that is credited as resulting in a noticeable increase in the number of those travelling by foot being injured and/or killed – around a 10 per cent increase in the United States, Britain and Australia since 2010. And this is despite the fact that this act is actually an offence according to most road laws.

I know I have nearly hit a couple of pedestrians who have walked on despite red lights, turning traffic and being old enough to know better. And despite their near brush with my car and me, these pedestrians were so immersed in their black mirrors they remained unaware of how close to danger they were, continuing on blissfully ignorant and self-immersed. This is despite the fact 1100-plus pedestrians are injured each year on Australian roads, with these figures rising rapidly.

In 2016, in-ground lights were installed at busy intersections in Sydney and Melbourne to stop mobile-phone zombies walking into oncoming traffic. This followed efforts of other major cities in regard to the same problem, such as Paris. After the deaths and injuries of 4500 pedestrians in traffic crashes in one year alone, the Road Safety Authority of Paris introduced a Virtual Crash Billboard at some of its danger hotspots.

When a pedestrian crosses while a light is red and a 'billboard' is present, the screeching sound of a car braking to avoid impact is heard and a photo of the jaywalker's reaction taken. These photos of pure terror are then displayed on billboards all over the city as a deterrent to others.

And frankly, I think it's time we investigate having the billboards installed here. Because something needs to change and it needs to happen now.

Or, perhaps we could go one further and follow China's lead. At a crossing in Daye, a city in the province of Hubei, police set up nifty machines that warn jaywalkers not to cross when the light is red. If they proceed, these contraptions spray water vapour at the pedestrians while photographing their reaction. These photographs are then displayed for others to see as well as being sent to police for recognition purposes.

Police report the machines are a real success and have saved lives, which makes sense considering the fear of potential water damage to precious phones may be the only way to actually motivate wexters to concentrate.

I am lucky. I do not have a love of my phone. In fact, I happily turn it off for long periods each day when I walk my dog, much to the constant annoyance of my friends. But I refuse to apologise. This is my/our precious time of carefree contemplation and exercise, a break to unwind and rewire. A time to turn off all the white noise and hear the birds instead. To listen to the jays, not behave like one.

Tips

- The writer generates a humorous tone at the beginning of the piece, with her opening anecdote followed by the self-deprecating description of herself as a 'cranky old woman'. She returns to this tone and this persona at the end of the piece, when she declares her refusal to apologise for turning off her phone and likens jaywalkers to chatty birds. In doing so, she hopes to present herself as likeable due to her frankness and principled stand.
- This forthrightness and relatability is furthered by her occasional use of casual and colloquial language such as 'mate' and 'nifty', as well as inclusive language, as in 'we simply do not exist' and 'our road rules'. The aim is to foster a connection between Squires and her readers as joint victims of irresponsible 'wexters'.
- Her tone shifts to informative with an element of humour as she explains jaywalking and the term 'wexter', before becoming serious as she presents statistics regarding the injuries and deaths resulting from this behaviour. These gradual shifts in tone allow her to make a serious argument, with some potentially distressing supporting points, less confronting for her readers, who are likely to have been disarmed by her conversational opening before having to take in the sobering facts and figures.
- References to international examples of wexting prevention in Paris and Daye are included to support Squires' call for similar measures in Australia. Wide-ranging precedents such as these convey the impression that other countries are ahead of Australia in tackling the problem, inciting a desire in readers to keep up with these progressive examples.

Scenario 19: Giving gifts, not things

Instructions

- In this section, you are required to analyse the use of argument(s) and language to persuade an intended audience to share the point of view expressed in an unseen persuasive text.
- Read the background information on this page and the material on the following pages, and write an analytical response to the task below.
- For the purposes of this task, the term 'language' refers to written and spoken language, and 'visuals' refers to images and graphics.
- This section is worth one-third of the total marks for the examination.

Task

Write an analysis of the ways in which argument(s), written and spoken language, and visuals are used in the material on the following pages to try to persuade the intended audience to share the point of view presented.

Background information

Athena and her large family have gathered for a Christmas meal together to exchange gifts. The following is a transcript of the speech Athena, a young professional woman, gave at the table while she handed out personalised cards to her family members. The image accompanying the text is a copy of the flyer Athena provided inside each card.

OK, well, since none of us could possibly eat another mouthful of Mum and Dad's festive meal, I've got something I'd like to say. First, merry Christmas to you all. I really love Christmas. It's not just about the food – though I have to say, Dad, this was your best custard yet! It's not just the traditional Lee family lawn bowls tournament (watch out, Uncle Rod, I've been practising!). Instead, as all the clichés say, Christmas is a time of giving.

This year, though, you've probably noticed that I didn't buy gifts for any of you – and not because I was disorganised. The real reason is that I've learned there are better ways to show my love for my family, and I'm trying to change my mindset. In each of your Christmas cards, you will find my present to you.

For some of you, I've made vouchers for things we can do together – I think they're called 'experience gifts'. (Spoiler: Gran, I'm finally taking you out for high tea.)

For some of you, I've made IOU vouchers for things I will do. This year I'll be weeding the garden (you're welcome, Mum); sewing (the twins will be the cutest-dressed kids at Morton Primary); and baking brownies (you're all hoping that's for you, right?!). Plus some other fun stuff.

But mostly, I've made contributions in your names to a bunch of different charities. I've thought really hard about them all, and chosen things that I hope will mean a lot to you. Hai, I think you will love knowing that your 'gift' this Christmas is school fees for a teenager in South Sudan. Jo (and Rover!), you'll be happy to know yours is a donation to RSPCA Victoria. Food banks, homeless shelters and medical aid all feature too.

Whether we are supporting communities and individuals close to home, or making connections with the global society we are part of, I think we have a responsibility to understand our privilege. I think we have a duty to share some of our financial and social wealth. Because most people aren't as lucky as we are in this family. In a country with free speech and a relatively functional healthcare system, we have plenty of food, we have jobs, we have homes, we have each other. But most of all, we have THINGS.
Too. Many. Things.

It's easier than ever these days to spend money buying STUFF we don't need. Even kids without credit cards can buy online using Afterpay and Zip. We can pretty much have whatever we want. But have you thought about your carbon footprint with all that online ordering? The environmental costs of production, marketing and transport? What about ethical sustainability? What about treatment of workers – do you know who made your new handbag or your latest tech gadget? Do you know if they were paid fairly?

And aside from the moral cost of things, you know you'll spend more online, even when it looks like a bargain at first. Think about those ridiculously high fees you have to pay because you've left it too late and need express postage!

Or maybe you're shopping in person and supporting local small business? Awesome. Do it. Love your work. But have you thought about the cost of petrol, public transport or parking? Have you realised you're wasting hours and hours of your life panicking and searching for that perfect present for someone who has everything? A perfect present, by the way, that doesn't exist.

That's it. I'm not buying stuff for presents anymore.

And hey, there are extra benefits for you guys too. Nobody has to pretend they don't already have the exact same Bluetooth speaker at home. Nobody has to pretend they enjoy apricot nougat when they really don't. You all know what I'm talking about.

I know families who use a Secret Santa app where everyone only has to buy one gift. Sure, that's pretty cool – it's fun, and it reduces the sheer volume of presents. It means nobody is left out by accident. And it cuts out the stress about how much money to spend on cousins you don't know very well, or how many presents to give your siblings. It even cuts out the worry about giving someone something they don't want – the apps let you request specific gifts! But where's the joy in that? It's just a blatant shopping list. It's greedy. It's disgusting. It's consumerism gone mad. And it's nothing to do with the true Christmas spirit.

So that's why you won't find boxes from me under the tree for you this year. I'm honestly not judging the rest of you for buying presents – presents aren't all bad. But this was my choice for this year, and I hope some of you consider making the same choice next time you want to buy something for someone. (In your cards I've included a little flyer for one of my favourite charities, if you want somewhere to start.) I hope you at least stop and think about whether the present you are giving is really heartfelt, personal and meaningful. If the answer is no, then remember that there are always other options. And if the answer is yes – or maybe if it's just a particularly awesome present – then go for it!

Now, let's get the lawn bowls going!

Tips

- The speaker's chatty, friendly and intimate tone is established immediately through the use of the casual words 'OK, well' to open her speech. This reflects her close relationship with her target audience, which consists of family members who are likely to be comfortable with and reassured by this familiar approach. References to shared family experiences such as her father's custard and the family lawn bowls tournament similarly draw on the existing relationship Athena has with her listeners, allowing her to present a potentially challenging idea in a non-threatening and warm way.
- The emphasis on shared experiences is continued throughout the speech, for instance in the references to Bluetooth speakers and apricot nougat; she states that her audience 'all know what I'm talking about' to convey the idea that receiving unwanted gifts is a universally relatable scenario. This enlists the audience on her side by assuming their preferences and interests are aligned.
- The speaker uses a series of rhetorical questions to invite listeners to reflect on the impact of their buying choices. This is also a gentler way of encouraging her audience to consider her points than using a series of blunter statements. Given that her listeners are family, this softer approach is likely to be better received than a more forceful or combative style of argument.
- Consider how the image echoes and reinforces the speaker's argument, taking a similar approach and tone. It includes the capitalised word 'THINGS', which is a word Athena also emphasises during her speech, and similarly uses a rhetorical question to encourage readers to reflect on their gift-giving choices.

Scenario 20: Beach lessons

Instructions

- In this section, you are required to analyse the use of argument(s) and language to persuade an intended audience to share the point of view expressed in an unseen persuasive text.
- Read the background information on this page and the material on the following pages, and write an analytical response to the task below.
- For the purposes of this task, the term 'language' refers to written and spoken language, and 'visuals' refers to images and graphics.
- This section is worth one-third of the total marks for the examination.

Task

Write an analysis of the ways in which argument(s), written and spoken language, and visuals are used in the material on the following pages to try to persuade the intended audience to share the point of view presented.

Background information

The following article appeared in *Child Monthly*, a magazine for parents of young children, widely distributed in maternal and child health centres. Zan Smith, a mother herself, responds to concerns about the increasing amount of time children spend viewing electronic media on television, computer, tablet and phone screens, as well as increasing rates of childhood obesity in Australia.

Beach lessons

By Zan Smith

During the long wet winter we've just had, our three toddlers were imprisoned in the house week after week, rarely able to escape for a run or a climb. Despite our best efforts to come up with activities and games, there was no end to the arguments and squabbling, or the constant demands for attention and novelty throughout the day.

Occasionally we resorted to the TV for half an hour or so of entertainment – and half an hour of peace and quiet in the house to get dinner prepared. But it always seemed to reduce them to a kind of inertia, stopping them from interacting with one another and from engaging in more active behaviours.

Although it freed me up to get something done, I never wanted it to go for more than an hour.

So I was very interested, and rather concerned, to read the article in the previous issue of *Child Monthly* on iPads and computers being used in classrooms from Prep onwards, to encourage kids to do their own learning and creative play – especially kids who are slow to read and write. I can't help wondering if this is all a bit too much too soon. Where is this all going? What will happen to our children when they are older, if interacting with a screen becomes so normal so early?

In the US, for instance, the Department of Health and Human Services has reported that 8- to 18-year-olds are watching hours a day of TV *and* spending at least an hour a day playing video games. When do these children do their homework? Read a book? Play sport?

Captivated by the screen – but how much is too much?

In Canada there are guidelines for the amount of activity young children should be doing, based on findings that children aged 4 and under are spending over 70% of their days being sedentary. These guidelines are also addressing alarming levels of childhood obesity, with around a quarter of Canadian children being overweight or obese.

Is this where we're heading in Australia, too? In a country where kids used to grow up playing sport for hours after school, either in organised competitions or impromptu games of backyard cricket? Or practically living at the beach all summer? It seems the answer is 'yes'. The Australian Bureau of Statistics reports that, in 2022, 27.7% of children aged 5 to 17 were overweight or obese.

And in Australia, too, authorities are recommending lower levels of screen time for young children. The Raising Children Network recommends no more than an hour a day of screen time for children between 2 and 5, and no more than two hours for children aged 5 and over.

It's not that screen time by itself is necessarily a bad thing, in the way that eating sugar is bad for your teeth. There are many educational games and apps that kids find fun and engaging, and which undoubtedly help them to learn. And digital literacy is going to be more and more important in our children's lives.

Rather, it's the things that are not happening while you're sitting or lying in front of a screen that make it essential to limit its use. It's the senses that aren't being engaged: while sight and sound are active, taste and smell are totally dormant. Touch can be used minimally for a tablet, but there is really nothing especially tactile about a glass screen, and we all know how much children learn by doing things with their hands.

It was a great relief to our family, then, when the warm weather finally arrived and we could set off for our local beach once again, buckets and spades, towels and togs in hand. Miraculously, the arguments and demands stopped almost instantly as the fresh air, the soft sand and the cool water provided all the stimulation needed for hours at a time. Sandcastles were built, races were run along the beach, faces were splashed. There were so many things to see and hear, but even more importantly there were things to taste, smell and – most of all – touch.

The beach can be much more than a playground; it's also a school for life.

I was amazed by the transformation in my children's behaviour, from cranky to content, from depending on me as the source of all entertainment and education to finding these things readily available on the beach. The beach is not just a playground; it's also a place where children learn without even trying. Marine and bird life are all around, from seagulls to tiny fish in the shallows to the tenacious mussels, limpets and crabs eking out an existence in rock pools. Playing with water and sand becomes a lesson in flow, absorption, textures. A surfboard left on the beach for communal use becomes a child's first ecstatic experience of buoyancy.

Even the hazards of the beach are instructive: the dangers of too much sun exposure; the risk posed by creatures that might bite or sting; the threat implicit in deep or rough water. All are part of life's complexity, yet become sources of learning and understanding when they are part of an environment we clearly belong to.

So here's looking forward to a long summer, to days on the beach, to swimming lessons – and, in all weathers, the open air, the world of the senses, and sources of childhood contentment that enrich all of our lives.

Tips

- As the opinion piece appears in a magazine called *Child Monthly*, its target audience can be presumed to consist primarily of parents. Reflect on the way in which the description of a winter spent indoors with squabbling children is likely to be familiar to such an audience, whose empathetic response to this scenario primes them to accept Smith's reflections on screen time.
- The emphasis on learning through outdoor play in the latter part of the piece capitalises on this receptivity, focusing on the assumed desire of most readers, given their interaction with a parenting magazine, to wish to maximise their children's educational experiences.
- The writer generates a reflective and lyrical tone through the use of carefully chosen words and phrases; for example, the words 'miraculously', 'transformation', 'amazed' and 'ecstatic', with their connotations of wonder and even the divine, help to paint an idyllic picture of children at play. Adjectives such as 'fresh', 'soft', 'cool' and 'warm' reinforce the benefits of tactile engagement with the beach environment that the writer extols, helping to evoke in the reader a strong desire for their own children to experience the same joy and developmental benefits of outdoor time.
- Note the way in which the two images are intended to work in tandem to present a 'before and after' scenario. The former shows the backs of two young children watching a screen; the fact that their faces aren't shown both suggests that screen overuse is a problem that is not specific to these particular children but experienced by many, and creates an impression of passivity and stagnancy, given their facial expressions cannot be seen. The lighting, too, is flat and the environment in which they are sitting is drab. In contrast, the latter photo shows two happy children actively engaged in building a sandcastle. They are active, rather than sitting still, and the environment around them is rich and stimulating.

Scenario 21: Don't ban the exam

Instructions

- In this section, you are required to analyse the use of argument(s) and language to persuade an intended audience to share the point of view expressed in an unseen persuasive text.
- Read the background information on this page and the material on the following pages, and write an analytical response to the task below.
- For the purposes of this task, the term 'language' refers to written and spoken language, and 'visuals' refers to images and graphics.
- This section is worth one-third of the total marks for the examination.

Task

Write an analysis of the ways in which argument(s), written and spoken language, and visuals are used in the material on the following pages to try to persuade the intended audience to share the point of view presented.

Background information

In response to a recent call from some parents and educators to stop using exams to assess students' skills in Year 12, university lecturer Bronwyn Leigh wrote the following opinion piece. Her piece was published in *Learning Now*, a monthly magazine aimed at teachers and other educational professionals.

Don't ban the exam

The exam: still a fair and accurate way to assess students.

Exams. The very word has struck fear into generations of students. I well remember sleepless pre-exam nights, the long, isolating rows of single tables and chairs and the initial panic that would temporarily blank out all knowledge of a subject as I opened the exam paper. Perhaps these recollections should make it easy for me to endorse recent calls to cease using examinations as a formal assessment tool for Year 12 students. However, I'm not so sure that other forms of assessment alone help us to adequately measure student knowledge and ability. I'm also not convinced by claims that exams are as outdated as some commentators would have us believe. Of course, I'm not suggesting that exams should be the sole form of student assessment in Year 12 – or, indeed, at any level – but I do believe that they have their place and that they enable assessors to gauge student learning in a fair and rigorous way. A balance between exams and other forms of assessment is what is needed to ensure deep learning and parity of assessment.

It is worth noting that the push to eradicate exams for Year 12 is supported by very little research. No doubt most of us can guess some of the claims made against exams: that they unfairly discriminate against bright students whose anxiety hinders their ability to do well; that they are an unnatural form of assessment because no one really has to work under exam pressure in the 'real world'; and that they allow for cramming[1] rather than deep learning experiences. There is a little merit in all of these claims – we all know of someone who didn't perform as well as they were expected to because they had a meltdown before walking into the exam room, for instance.

But these claims alone do not justify calls to abandon a form of assessment that has been reliably used in education since the mid-nineteenth century. And all of these claims can actually be used to promote exams rather than to condemn them. If students panic before exams, they need to be taught how to cope with stressful situations, because they are, like it or not, part and parcel of everyday life. In fact, many people do have to work under exam-like pressure in the 'real world': imagine being a doctor in the emergency section of a hospital and having to say to a bloodied, distraught accident victim, 'hang on while I check my reference book'. Imagine being a teacher and regularly needing to say, 'I'll get back to you on that one' in response to student questions. And, as for cramming, well, I'd rather students cram for the moment and learn something than do nothing and learn nothing. Students who can't be bothered to prepare properly for exams are unlikely to be enthusiastic about alternative forms of assessment: at least exams give them the opportunity to focus their energies for a relatively short amount of time.

One of the alternatives suggested to replace exams is a research thesis that students could work on throughout the year. The thesis would form a major component of a student's end-of-year mark, alongside usual class-based assessments. There is no doubt that engaging in such a project would allow students to develop all-important research, analytical and writing skills, regardless of the subject area. But there are a number of issues that make me sceptical about its suitability as an alternative to exams. If students needed to write, say, a 10 000-word thesis for every subject, they would have very little time for their class-based studies. I also wonder how such theses – which are by their very nature highly individual pieces of research and writing – could be marked fairly and consistently for all students. And if they were marked solely by the students' teachers, what is to stop schools from exploiting the system? Even at university most students do not write a formal research-based thesis until their honours year, so it seems unreasonable to expect Year 12 students to rise to the task and for schools to have the resources to help every student achieve their best.

It is true that exams alone are not an ideal way to assess students, but in conjunction with other forms of assessment they provide a useful tool for accurately measuring student performance on a given day. My own recollections of exams are not always positive ones; nevertheless, my experience as both a student and an educator tells me that exams have their place and should not be relegated to the dustbin of history.

Bronwyn Leigh has lectured in education studies at a number of universities for more than thirty years.

[1]**cramming** – quickly memorising facts immediately before an exam

Tips

- The writer acknowledges the drawbacks of exams, for instance when she refers to her own 'panic' at exams as a student and when she concedes that they are 'not an ideal way to assess students'. This serves to establish her as balanced and reasonable in her approach to the issue by suggesting that she has considered multiple angles and arrived at her viewpoint via reasoned consideration.
- The scenarios presented by Leigh – of a doctor needing to check a reference book before treating an accident victim and a teacher unable to answer students' questions – aim to alarm readers with the potential real-world consequences of not assessing students via exams. The emotive description of the doctor's patient as 'bloodied' and 'distraught' targets readers' sympathy and also their self-interest, as no one would like to be in the position of the patient under the care of an ill-informed doctor.
- Leigh's overall approach is to acknowledge that exams are 'not an ideal' form of assessment but also to lay out all the ways in which, despite this, they are still useful and ought to be kept. She does this by suggesting that many of the criticisms of exams could actually be looked at as advantages – for example, they can teach students how to manage stress. She also argues that alternative methods, such as a thesis, have even more disadvantages than exams, presenting a worst-case-scenario description of a lengthy thesis requirement that would leave students little time for class-based study and raise issues of inequitable grading. The intention is to encourage readers to agree that, whatever criticisms they might have of exams, they ought to accept them as there is no good alternative.

SCENARIO 22: Betta fish

Instructions

- In this section, you are required to analyse the use of argument(s) and language to persuade an intended audience to share the point of view expressed in an unseen persuasive text.
- Read the background information on this page and the material on the following pages, and write an analytical response to the task below.
- For the purposes of this task, the term 'language' refers to written and spoken language, and 'visuals' refers to images and graphics.
- This section is worth one-third of the total marks for the examination.

Task

Write an analysis of the ways in which argument(s), written and spoken language, and visuals are used in the material on the following pages to try to persuade the intended audience to share the point of view presented.

Background information

Animal rights activists have long criticised pet shops for their treatment of fish, accusing them of shipping fish in cramped and cruel conditions and not caring for them when they arrive. However, many aquarium forums support pet shops as ethical places to buy pet fish, claiming that the fish are transported safely.

Bettas (also known as Siamese fighting fish) don't require filters or air pumps in their aquariums and are classified as easy pets to care for, which leads to them being one of the most popular and most often mistreated fish.

The following pages feature a blog post by a mother, Rowena Soto, sharing her negative experience of buying fish in a pet shop. It appeared on her personal blog, EcoMums.

Betta fish deserve betta!

So I've just been to the chain pet shop in town and I am *livid*. I've been thinking lately about getting my son a Betta, but after what I just saw I'm never going back there again!

First, they weren't even in proper tanks! Each fish was in a tiny plastic cup with hardly any room to swim or move around. They all had murky water and the poor fish were practically stacked on top of each other. A lot of them looked sick, and as far as I could tell some of them were already dead. Even my five-year-old could tell at a glance that something was wrong, asking me in a trembling voice, 'Are the fish okay, Mum?'

Of course, I hurried him away from the distressing sight, mumbling something vaguely reassuring. But the fact is, the fish are definitely *not* okay.

What are these pet shops thinking?!

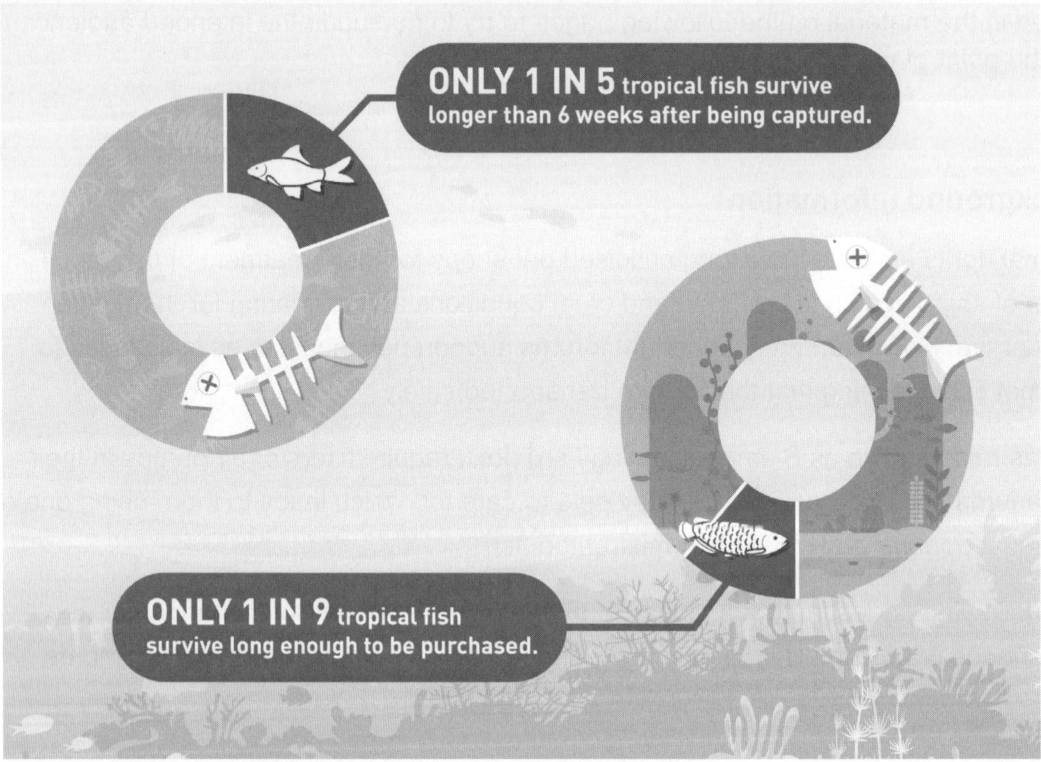

Source: https://forthefishes.org/

I tried to find someone I could talk to, but of course there were only two people working that I could see. When I complained that the fish were living in such horrible conditions, the employee just shrugged and said there was nothing he could do. Apparently they have so many other important things to take care of in this tiny pet shop that no one has time to even change the water. And on top of that, he couldn't even answer me when I pestered him about why those beautiful fish were kept in plastic prisons.

I tracked down the other employee and asked him what he knew about keeping tropical fish, and he had absolutely zero knowledge on caring for a Betta. That's when I demanded to speak to the manager, but of course she was 'not in today' so I was given a corporate phone number to call to make my complaint. The staff were completely uninterested in my concerns, not that I entirely blame them for their ignorance and apathy. Clearly, this lack of interest in the welfare of the animals in their care came from management. This was not a one-off 'mistake' but a systemic issue that spoke volumes about the shop owner's passion for profit, not pets.

It horrifies me to think how many people have gone in and purchased fish with absolutely no idea how to care for them. And what bothered me just as much as the incompetent 'pet care' staff were the products being sold in the shop.

There were quite a few tanks that were labelled as aquariums for Bettas, but they were disgustingly small. Some were even designed to house several together, with nothing but a piece of plastic to keep them separated. As one of the most aggressive fish you can buy, male Bettas should not be able to see other males every second of the day, with nowhere to hide. It would be sure to cause an insane amount of stress on the fish, and stressed fish are very likely to get sick and die. Imagine being trapped in a tiny space with creatures liable to attack you at any time and no means of defending or shielding yourself. There is simply no justification for submitting any creature – no matter how small – to such psychological torment.

In the end, like my child, I had to turn away. I just couldn't believe it!

These pet shops are only concerned about one thing: money. They think that by marketing Bettas as easy pets to care for with these cute small tanks, they can make more sales. What happens to these fish after they leave the shop is clearly no concern of the owner pocketing the cash for every ill-informed sale.

After seeing those gorgeous fish in their little cups, I started to wonder if they were treated just as badly before they got to the shop. A quick internet search showed me that I was right. The fish are packed into cardboard boxes in miniscule plastic bags with a very tiny amount of water, and many of them die on the journey.

I could only stomach looking at the pictures for a few minutes before I had to turn away. Fish feel pain, people! It's been scientifically proven, and we need to help them.

So I'm asking all of my friends and followers to follow my example and never buy from pet shops again. How can a company claim to love animals when their fish are dying in transit, on the shelves and in the homes of ignorant buyers?

I almost went back to the shop to buy their whole stock of Bettas so I could rescue them, but realised there would only be new fish brought in and left to starve and rot in their own filth. I hope everyone else feels my disgust, and joins me in boycotting these unethical shops. If we don't support pet shops, hopefully they'll leave those poor Bettas alone. And you can bet I'll be calling that corporate number every day until something gets done!

Tips

- The writer generates a distressed and angry tone through such vocabulary choices as 'livid', 'horrifies' and 'disgustingly'. Such terms help to evoke similar emotions in the reader, who is thus positioned to share the writer's outrage at pet shops and their treatment of fish.
- The writer compounds this with the use of exclamation marks and rhetorical questions that aid in expressing her distress about the welfare of the fish she observed by clearly communicating her heightened emotions.
- The writer contrasts her emotional reaction with the 'apathy' of the chain pet shop and its staff: she describes them as ignorant and uncaring, with an absent manager and a 'passion for profit, not pets'. This contrast helps create an 'us and them' situation, with the writer encouraging her 'friends and followers' to align with her compassionate, more ethical point of view about the treatment of fish and to boycott the 'unethical shops'.
- While the writer's primary persuasive strategy is to target her readers' sympathy and anger, she bolsters this with some evidence to support her claims of poor treatment and ignorance on the part of pet shops; for example, when she refers to her 'quick internet search' and presents facts about Betta fish, this suggests she is well-informed on the topic. The effect is to convey to readers that her outrage is well-founded.
- The graphic included with the written text reflects this primarily emotive approach, presenting stark images of live fish alongside fish skeletons to visually present the high proportion of tropical fish deaths after capture. The statistics accompanying these images are equally stark and again reflect the writer's approach of justifying her distress with reference to facts and figures.

Scenario 23: Bookless libraries

Instructions

- In this section, you are required to analyse the use of argument(s) and language to persuade an intended audience to share the point of view expressed in an unseen persuasive text.
- Read the background information on this page and the material on the following pages, and write an analytical response to the task below.
- For the purposes of this task, the term 'language' refers to written and spoken language, and 'visuals' refers to images and graphics.
- This section is worth one-third of the total marks for the examination.

Task

Write an analysis of the ways in which argument(s), written and spoken language, and visuals are used in the material on the following pages to try to persuade the intended audience to share the point of view presented.

Background information

The principal of Romeo Road Secondary School, Petrov Price, writes a blog titled 'From the Principal's Corner' on the school website. He recently published the following post on the topic of bookless libraries.

ROMEO ROAD
SECONDARY SCHOOL

HOME ABOUT STUDENTS PARENTS **BLOG** CONTACT

BLOG > From the Principal's Corner

Looking back on my childhood, I have fond memories of my school library. Endless corridors lined with shelves, creaking wooden floors, cosy corners and books – so many books! There was something sacred about that building – something magical – and it came from being close to so many ideas, so much collected knowledge.

Today, however, knowledge looks a little different from when I was growing up. The new generation of digital natives associates ideas with the click of a mouse, or the results of a search, rather than the pages between two cloth boards. Which leaves school libraries like the one I used as a child – products of the paper age – facing some difficult questions.

What does the library for the digital age look like?

What does it do? And who is it for?

Romeo Road library is also facing these questions. Since its founding in 1945, our school has prided itself on being at the forefront of change. Ours was one of the first schools in the country to introduce the PC to classrooms in the late 1980s; we have since led the way in adopting new technologies, from BYO[1] devices to our e-learning platform.

But despite our efforts to bring this school into the twenty-first century, our library remains firmly stuck in the nineteenth. Apart from a lone computer lab, it continues to function as a place to house physical books – a notion that is now as outdated as the atlas[2] (remember those?), and just about as useful to our students. (Records show that students checked out just 45 books this month.) For my part, I believe it's time we close the book on Romeo Road library's dark ages – and the first step is getting rid of our collection of paper books altogether.

A library without books? It's controversial, sure – but it's not *that* controversial. Around the world, libraries are reading the writing on the screen and phasing out physical books in favour of digitised collections and electronic subscription services. At its heart, the move towards 'bookless' is about making information as quickly, easily and widely accessible as possible. Finding what you need in a traditional library means searching for the book you're looking for (or asking a librarian), taking it to the counter, checking it out and returning it; reading the ebook version of a publication, however, is as simple as searching an electronic catalogue on a device and hitting download.

And despite the term, a bookless library would actually give students access to more books than they have ever had before – including leading magazines, journals and newspapers from around the world. Phasing out physical books also has a number of other benefits, including reducing the cost to an institution.

As principal, I can tell you that managing a collection of physical books is an expensive exercise: paper books require a significant amount of space and maintenance, and printed information can quickly become outdated. Ebooks, on the other hand, are cheaper than their hard-copy counterparts and accessible from anywhere with a login and an internet connection. Removing physical books and their shelves from the Romeo Road library would also create a lot of extra space, and this kind of real estate could be put to good use – in the form of extra computer labs, for example; a space for people to create things; or even a digital recording studio.

An additional benefit of bookless libraries that became very apparent during Covid times is that they are obviously far more hygienic. Passing any kind of physical object from hand to hand, particularly one as prone to collecting dirt and germs as a book, is just an extra avenue of risk that there seems no good reason to take if we don't have to.

Moreover – another relief for busy parents! – no borrowing of physical books means no more having to constantly remind your children to return them.

As parents and educators, it's easy to be nostalgic about libraries such as the ones we grew up with. But those libraries belonged to a world that no longer exists. Our children feel very differently about the best way to gather and store vast amounts of information, and our chief purpose here is to meet their needs and help to fit them for a digital future that will look vastly different from the one imagined when we were young.

I know how upsetting the idea of a library without books will be for some people, but to my mind the choice is clear: either we turn the page on the physical book now, or we end up having to do it later anyway. The world is changing, and Romeo Road needs to be changing with it – for the sake of our school and, most importantly, our students.

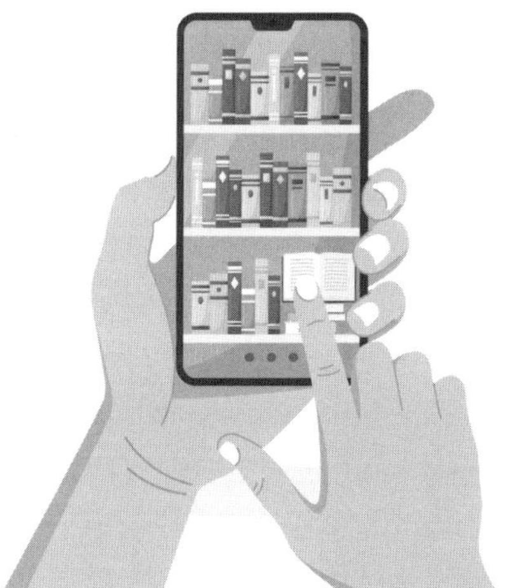

[1]**BYO** – bring your own
[2]**atlas** – a book containing a collection of maps

Tips

- Think about how the text's presentation – appearing on a school-branded website beneath a banner with the school name and logo on it – might affect how readers receive the principal's message, particularly as they are likely to be parents of students at Romeo Road Secondary School.
- Why might the principal open with a fond, nostalgic recollection of the library of his childhood? How might this connect him to readers and prepare them for his ultimate stance on removing physical books from the school library?
- Consider how the principal closely relates his supporting reasons and persuasive techniques to his main argument – that digitising the library is, above all, for the benefit of the students. For example, his rhetorical questions – 'What does the library for the digital age look like? … And who is it for?' – gently remind readers that, although they might have sentimental or nostalgic feelings regarding physical books in libraries, just as he himself does, this is not necessarily helpful to 'the new generation of digital natives'. Similarly, his appeal to keeping up to date and avoiding having a library 'as outdated as the atlas' is supported with the fact that 'students checked out just 45 books this month' – evidence that contemporary students do not rely upon physical books in the same way that his generation did.
- The image the principal has chosen to include with his blog entry shows a phone screen featuring an image of bookshelves stacked with books. The suggestion is that this handheld device has the capacity to contain a large number of books, thus offering students the opportunity to read many different publications in a convenient, portable format. Consider how this might help to ease the fears of parents concerned that a bookless library might negatively affect their children's literacy and access to information.

Scenario 24: Colonising Mars

Instructions

- In this section, you are required to analyse the use of argument(s) and language to persuade an intended audience to share the point of view expressed in an unseen persuasive text.
- Read the background information on this page and the material on the following pages, and write an analytical response to the task below.
- For the purposes of this task, the term 'language' refers to written and spoken language, and 'visuals' refers to images and graphics.
- This section is worth one-third of the total marks for the examination.

Task

Write an analysis of the ways in which argument(s), written and spoken language, and visuals are used in the material on the following pages to try to persuade the intended audience to share the point of view presented.

Background information

The following article on why we should invest in establishing a colony on Mars was first published on Science is Super, a website aimed at making important scientific research, and opinions relating to scientific developments, accessible to a general audience. The author, Natasha O'Meara, is a scientist and she is a regular contributor to the website.

Three big reasons to colonise Mars – number three might surprise you!

By Natasha O'Meara

Mars holds a special place in our collective psyche. Books, films and TV shows have all grappled with the idea of an interstellar calling, a fundamental need to go beyond the confines of our current home for the sake of our species. The lure of Mars is undeniable. So why deny it?

Some of the greatest minds of their age, from Stephen Hawking to Carl Sagan, have expressed their support for colonising Mars. At a recent meeting in Houston, the centre of space research, sixty prominent scientists who are experts in their fields reached a similar conclusion: colonising Mars isn't just a wild idea or a project for the distant future; it's a necessity, a vital step for humanity to take.

Of course, it's understandable there's a certain reluctance to commit to a project like this. The cost could be in the billions, trillions even, a scale of spending that's difficult to comprehend for most people. Why not spend this money on tangibly improving the lives of people now, instead of on some far-off goal that won't help anyone for a long time, if it does at all?

But Mars missions would have practical benefits now and well into the future. Here are three reasons humans should colonise Mars.

1. The future of our species could depend on it

Experts agree that relying solely on Earth to sustain and maintain our continued existence is a recipe for disaster. The reality is that humans have been on Earth for a fraction of its existence: the blink of an eye, in a cosmic sense. Even with our limited knowledge, history is littered with examples of species coming and going; the dinosaurs, for instance, were wiped out by an asteroid.

If we could escape our home planet, however, we would drastically increase our chances of survival. And this wouldn't just safeguard against external threats like asteroids. It would also prevent us from destroying the only planet we have ever called home.

And the best part is, we don't even need to go trawling through galaxies trillions of light years away, desperately searching for somewhere habitable; Mars is right next door. Many scientists agree that Mars would make a perfect place for sustained human life; it meets many of the criteria we would want our future home to meet. By colonising it, we would guarantee that the human race will endure. And if we know all this, is there any reason not to devote our resources to doing so?

2. There could be alien life

Have you ever contemplated the existence of aliens? I think almost all of us, at one point or another, have wondered what it would be like to discover tangible proof of alien life. It would represent perhaps the most important scientific breakthrough of all time.

Of course, to properly search for life on Mars, it's vital that we get people up there. While it can be tempting to assume that we're better off letting robots do our dirty work, in reality humans are far better suited to discovery than even the best spacecraft explorers. If we want to plumb Mars' depths for its secrets, we've got to start getting people there.

There's even conjecture that life on Earth originated on Mars. Scientists have suggested that life may have come here from there via interstellar debris, such as rocks. These rocks may have contained early life and, thrown from their original home, come to Earth.

Unfortunately, there's been no concrete evidence found on our planet to support this theory. If anything, however, this just intensifies the need to properly explore Mars. While we have yet to see signs of extraterrestrial life, there's every reason to think that we're simply looking in the wrong place – or planet.

3. It could materially benefit life on Earth now

Instead of being a distraction from bettering life for everyone on Earth, efforts to colonise Mars would provide substantial benefits for our day-to-day lives here and now. That's because extending the limits of our horizons and striding forth into space are likely to lead to discoveries that will improve life on Earth. Pouring resources into the colonisation of Mars needn't be thought of in terms of how it might one day help us; it can benefit us much more immediately. Scientific history is full of examples of such breakthroughs.

Take, for instance, the microwave. Originally called the Radarange, the microwave's invention stems from an accident. A radar technician experimenting with electromagnetic waves stumbled upon an incredible discovery – these electromagnetic waves could be used to heat food. A now indispensable household item was the result of advancements in a seemingly unrelated field.

It's one of many life-changing discoveries that have come about as a result of humanity's drive to push itself to its limits. This story perfectly demonstrates the overlap between various fields; advancements in one area invariably benefit many others.

Moreover, not only will these advancements likely be beneficial to our health and wellbeing, they also provide us with fuel for our hopes and dreams. As demonstrated by the growing number of scientists investing time and effort into making the colonisation of Mars a reality, the prospect of being part of future space expeditions is exciting many. This could prompt future generations to take a similar interest, increasing the number of talented individuals dedicating their time to helping secure humanity's future.

The above reasons should illustrate why it's vital we commit now to going to Mars. The benefits are undeniable. So why wait?

Tips

- The background information indicates that this material is published online. Note how the writer uses a typical 'clickbait' strategy in the title of her piece, stating that 'number three might surprise you'. This is designed to encourage people to click on the article and read through to the end to discover the allegedly surprising 'big reason'. This strategy also supports the targeting of a broad audience interested in, yet mostly not experts in, science.
- The image centres on a human form on a different planet, illustrating the colonisation of Mars that Natasha O'Meara thinks is necessary. Consider the impact of using an image that only shows the back of the human, rather than the face. This enables the author to position the colonisation as a purely human endeavour, rather than one specific to a particular race or gender. Readers, regardless of their background, are thus able to envisage themselves as being in that spacesuit on Mars. In this case, the absence of specific identifying physical features in the photograph assists O'Meara in appealing to a wider audience.
- Consider the effect of O'Meara's ordering of the reasons for colonising Mars, and how these reasons work to position readers. As noted above, the title suggests that the third reason is the most significant, and it is certainly the most tangible and relatable to readers. The first two reasons are more aspirational or future-focused – while the survival of the human race and the possibility of alien life may attract keen scientists, an actual present-day benefit to life has the potential to connect with a wider audience.
- The article is published on Science is Super, so consider the target audience. Given the specific focus of the website, it is likely that the majority of readers have an existing interest in, and knowledge of, science. However, the article is not aimed at an intellectual or highly specific audience, as the language and content are still straightforward and accessible. Note how O'Meara includes references to two well-known scientists, Stephen Hawking and Carl Sagan, who are likely to be familiar to and considered reputable by readers.

Scenario 25: Vegan shoes

Instructions

- In this section, you are required to analyse the use of argument(s) and language to persuade an intended audience to share the point of view expressed in an unseen persuasive text.
- Read the background information on this page and the material on the following pages, and write an analytical response to the task below.
- For the purposes of this task, the term 'language' refers to written and spoken language, and 'visuals' refers to images and graphics.
- This section is worth one-third of the total marks for the examination.

Task

Write an analysis of the ways in which argument(s), written and spoken language, and visuals are used in the material on the following pages to try to persuade the intended audience to share the point of view presented.

Background information

Veganism is widely promoted as a healthy, ethical and environmentally conscious lifestyle choice. Some people argue, though, that not all vegan products are ethically superior to their non-vegan alternatives.

The following article exploring the issue of vegan shoes was written by Tanner Bowden. He is a staff writer for the New York–based lifestyle magazine *Gear Patrol*.

If you think your vegan shoes are saving the planet, you're wrong

By Tanner Bowden

I have beef[1] with vegan shoes.

Let me be clear, though – I think vegans are heroes. Their personal choice not to consume animal products is literally saving the world. Veganism is hard, too. I know this because after watching the popular (though rightly criticized) documentary *The Game Changers*, which extols the benefits of a vegan diet for athletic performance, I gave it a shot for a few weeks. I wanted to see how a short-term switch would make me feel, and how difficult it would be (good, difficult, though not as much as I'd imagined). So no, my problem is not with vegans – it's with vegan shoes.

Vegan leather shoes from mushroom mycelium and samples of vegan bio leather.

How can a shoe be vegan anyway? Simply put, it has to be completely free of animal products. That includes leather, wool and fur, as well as some glues that have animal-based ingredients in them (typically, it's collagen). Some definitions go further, insisting that any materials developed with animal testing must be excluded too.

Vegan shoes are becoming increasingly easier to find. The online retailer Zappos has a vegan filter that shows hundreds of options from brands like OluKai, Saucony, Merrell, Dr. Martens and more. Adidas recently revealed a vegan version of its popular Stan Smith shoe, the first iteration of which was a collaboration with Stella McCartney.

If lessening animal cruelty is the primary motivation behind your veganism, these shoes achieve that goal. But if general sustainability is the aim – and nearly every vegan shoe comes with a message that it's greener and better for the environment – the situation is messier.

The problem is that faux leather and fur are often made of synthetic, petroleum-based materials like polyvinyl chloride (PVC) and polyurethane (PU). Essentially, they're plastic. Technically, the cheap plastic-and-foam flip flops that wash up on beaches around the world are 'vegan'. Plus, in pursuing a degree of similarity that'll make people want to wear these shoes, companies often apply harmful chemicals that make them look and bend and wear just like the real deal.

OluKai is one brand that acknowledges the issue, though many don't. In a blog post on its site explaining vegan shoes, the brand notes: 'It's important to remember that animal-free shoes are not always more "environmentally friendly" by default … It is a lengthy and contentious debate as to whether leather production or synthetic production is worse for the environment.' It does note too, however, that vegan shoes are 'generally considered to leave a smaller carbon footprint'. Most companies making vegan shoes are content to greenwash over such nuance.

This conundrum calls to mind the recent implementation of plastic straw bans. I watched cafes react to it in New York City, some of them opting for paper replacements though many went for sippy lids made of plastic. Some are recyclable, supposedly, though good luck finding a recycling bin in Manhattan.

Some cafes and cities were better equipped for the ban than New York, and some companies make vegan alternatives more responsibly than others. Leather provides the best examples: an Italian company called Frumat makes it partially out of apples, while Piñatex is leather made of pineapple leaves. Mushroom-based leather is also a thing (and both Adidas and Stella McCartney will be its earliest adopters). It's promising stuff, but none of these faux leathers are being produced at a scale approaching that of the petroleum-based alternatives.

Meanwhile, is genuine leather really so bad? Again, advocates for animal rights will answer yes. From a sustainability perspective, the issue lies in the tanning process, which produces wastewater sludge with high concentrations of harmful chemicals like chromium and glutaraldehyde. Not only is it bad for the environment, but it's dangerous for workers.

But leather production is getting eco-friendlier too. It's a byproduct of the meat industry, for starters, and beef farmers aren't going to stop raising beef cows simply because they can't sell their skins (unless way more people adopt vegan diets, that is). Vegetable tanning uses organic material instead of chromium to preserve the skins, and some companies like Ecco are developing dry tanning methods that eliminate water waste. There's even a group of brands, retailers and producers that aims to hold the industry to a set of environmental protocols.

The best example of sustainably produced leather footwear comes, unsurprisingly, from Patagonia. In late 2020, the company released the Wild Idea Work Boot, made of bison leather with a Goodyear welt so the outsole can be replaced years into its life. The hides come from the same animals that it harvests to make its buffalo jerky – they are raised in a manner that restores the grasslands and promotes carbon sequestration[2]. Previously unused, the hides are tanned with olive tree leaves. What's more, Patagonia is only making as many boots as it has enough leather for (so good luck getting a pair).

It is true that Patagonia's bison boot model doesn't scale, but neither does the mushroom leather option (at least, not yet). Sustainability is complicated, and it can feel paralyzing when it seems like every option is bad.

There is hope, though – both vegan and non-vegan footwear is getting more sustainable. And, recently, Adidas and Allbirds announced that they are putting competition aside to create a performance shoe with the smallest carbon footprint ever. Given that the latter brand's signature ingredient is wool, chances are it won't be vegan.

[1]**have beef** – to have an issue with
[2]**carbon sequestration** – removing carbon dioxide from the atmosphere, either naturally (plants) or artificially

Tips

- Note how the writer engages the audience by using a conversational tone in the opening paragraphs. From the humorous use of the word 'beef' (employing a second meaning of the word) to the inclusion of his personal experience of, and response to, veganism, Bowden immediately softens any negativity that may have been aroused by the implied criticism in the title of the article. Both vegan and non-vegan readers are welcomed in this discussion. The tone then shifts to become more informative as Bowden introduces specific evidence to support his argument.
- Discuss the structure of the article. Bowden begins by defining vegan shoes then acknowledges the common perception of veganism as a 'healthy, ethical and environmentally conscious lifestyle choice' (quote taken from the background information). He points out that, for many vegans, 'lessening animal cruelty' by aiming for 'general sustainability' is the 'primary motivation' behind their veganism. The problem with this position is suggested by the article's title, in which Bowden argues that it might be 'wrong' to assume that 'vegan shoes are saving the planet'. The article then explains why faux leather and fur are problematic and goes on to discuss some genuinely sustainable alternatives. After exploring these options and establishing that there is a problem with scale, Bowden suggests that if the central desire is to save the planet then sustainable animal leather may in fact be a more viable option. Consider how readers, particularly vegan readers, might respond to this suggestion.
- Consider the impact of the inclusion of particular brand names, many of which are quite 'high-end' labels – Stella McCartney, Adidas, Patagonia. What does the writer achieve by citing such well-known and well-respected designers? Consider the implied contrast between the brands that are described as being 'content to greenwash' and OluKai, which openly acknowledges the challenges.
- Explore how the image supports the idea that vegan shoes are considered 'greener and better for the environment'. The shoes in the background of the image have a very leather-like appearance, supporting Bowden's statement that manufacturers often try to make their vegan leather 'look and bend and wear just like the real deal'. The inclusion of natural and environmentally sensitive products around the shoes – mushrooms and samples of vegan leather – adds to the impression that these shoes are natural and environmentally sustainable. The image resembles a promotional photo, which implicitly illustrates the writer's argument that vegan shoes are often marketed as 'greener and better for the environment' despite the 'lengthy and contentious debate' about this claim.

SAMPLE RESPONSES

Sample response 1: Life skills in schools

Inspired by concerns around their preparedness for life beyond school, the Student Representative Council at Olympus High School has published an open letter. Targeting an audience of fellow Olympus High students, the letter encourages students to sign a petition that will be presented to the school board, requesting that the school offers life skills classes. The letter includes two images: a meme and a photograph.

The council begins by stating the purpose of the open letter and outlining the current situation. By opening with a focus on the negative, with the use of the rule of threes in the repetition of 'something is wrong', it presents the current situation as concerning, encouraging the reader to feel a sense of urgency in resolving the issue. The letter references well-known topics in certain school subjects such as 'Pythagoras' theorem', 'mitochondria [being] the powerhouse of the cell' and 'the steps to the Nutbush', which would be familiar to many in the student audience, alongside alternative, real-world skills such as 'how to lodge a tax return', 'how to manage conflict' and 'ways to cope with stress'. By directly contrasting what is currently taught with authentic life skills, the council seeks to imply the inadequacies of the education system, encouraging students to question whether the content they are learning is actually relevant to real life. The first image, depicting a simple square and circle with the caption 'Thank goodness for geometry in school instead of tax class. Really helped this year when I had to pay my shapes' further mocks the irrelevance of curriculum content by highlighting its lack of use in the real world. This image, in the form of a meme, aims to connect with the student audience through the familiarity of the form, and its use of humour emphasises a serious point. The letter continues to emphasise that skills are of greater significance than content, as it moves on to reference the Australian Curriculum and how it is 'expected that students will develop skills in self-management and relationship building'. It notes that 'the government recognises the importance' of these things, before questioning 'so why doesn't Olympus High?' By highlighting that skill-building is part of the national curriculum, while stating bluntly that it is not being offered at their school, the council implies that Olympus High is failing to prepare its students, and that something needs to be done, thus positioning readers to sign the petition so that it may influence the board.

Having introduced the issue, the council moves on to outline its proposal – that life skills classes should be offered at Olympus High. Employing a logical approach, which acknowledges the challenges of timetabling, the letter suggests that classes 'could be held at lunchtime', and that 'each class would be led by a teacher from a different study area'. These points aim to reassure students – and also any parents who read the letter – who may be concerned that class time could be lost, or specific subjects impacted. The reference to existing teachers also aims to create a sense of familiarity, as these skills would be delivered by people with whom students already have a relationship, which may encourage them to feel comfortable and trusting about the sessions.

To support the proposal further, the letter next provides external support for its proposition, arguing that psychology experts and parents both agree that life skills should be taught. Statistics from noted mental health organisations Mission Australia and the Black Dog Institute are presented to demonstrate that there is significant research behind the proposal. The positive benefits of stress management are presented in the embedded photograph, which depicts two young people practising yoga. Their calm appearance and positive expressions suggest that they are successfully employing 'strategies for dealing with stress and anxiety', positioning students to consider the fact that they too could benefit if such strategies were taught at Olympus High. Parental support for the idea of life skills being taught in schools is then emphasised, with further research from the reputable institution Monash University included to illustrate this. The traditional role of parents teaching their children such life skills is raised, but then rebutted, as the letter acknowledges the increased demands on parents and the prevalence of families in which both parents work. This positions students to reflect on their own family situation, and to consider whether their parents have time to teach them these skills. Additionally, as the letter may be read by some parents, this seeks to gain their support for the proposal as well, by acknowledging that parents are time-poor, and providing a solution that still enables their children to be well prepared to face their future.

The council closes its letter with a call to action, encouraging students to sign the petition and make a difference. It references both students and parents, acknowledging the important role that both play when it comes to education, before setting a clear timeline for signing the petition. By highlighting that 'the school board meets' next month, the council returns the letter to the tone of the first paragraphs, suggesting there is a sense of urgency to the issue, thus positioning readers to sign immediately.

Sample response 2: Greenwashing

Speaking at an expo on ethical consumerism, environmental advocate Makena Green-Moore highlights the challenges of shopping sustainably by criticising the behaviour of unethical businesses. Targeting an audience of people either already committed to, or interested in, ethical consumerism, she contends that big businesses are guilty of 'greenwashing' to hide their unethical and unsustainable behaviour. Through her presentation, delivered in a friendly and assured tone, Green-Moore encourages listeners to be more mindful when shopping, to help build 'a more environmentally friendly and sustainable community'.

Green-Moore begins by contextualising the issue, introducing the concept of 'greenwashing' to her audience. Before doing this, however, she opens with an Acknowledgement of Country, recognising the Aboriginal and Torres Strait Islander owners of the land where the expo is being held. While this is increasingly a common feature at the beginning of many Australian presentations, her use of it here positions her as socially conscious from the outset of her speech, and she builds on this throughout her presentation. Moving to focus on the issue specifically, she depicts a shopping scenario that would be familiar to many listeners, encouraging them to imagine themselves in the same situation. With her opening scenario having been presented in a gentle manner, her jarring emphasis on the word 'WRONG!' seeks to shock listeners, highlighting that ethical consumerism is not as simple as initially indicated. The audience is positioned to question whether they have 'been subject to "greenwashing"', but Green-Moore reassures her listeners that, if they have, it isn't their fault, by attributing blame instead to 'unethical marketing' by 'clever manufacturers'. This introduces the concept of big businesses being the villains in this issue, and positions the audience to see manufacturers as being to blame for the challenges of ethical consumerism. Green-Moore continues by listing a number of seemingly environmentally-friendly phrases, such as 'all natural', 'raw' and 'plant-based', which her audience may be familiar with. This, again, encourages listeners to consider whether they have been tricked by marketers, and positions them to view such companies negatively, and thus be receptive to Green-Moore's suggestions about how to buy ethically.

Having presented a negative picture of the actions of manufacturers, Green-Moore changes to a more optimistic tone, highlighting that corporations are finally being held accountable for their behaviour. By providing an example focused on Coca-Cola – one of the biggest and most well-known corporations in the world – being taken to court, Green-Moore seeks to give confidence to her listeners, by showing that even big companies can be punished if they mislead their customers. Building on her previous discussion of the misleading language employed by marketers, the speaker provides an example specific to Coca-Cola, depicting the company as 'falsely advertising' itself as environmentally concerned, despite being 'the largest plastic polluter in the world'. By revealing that Coke was apparently using 'plant plastic' for its bottles, Green-Moore positions the manufacturer to be seen as deceitful and manipulative, implying that there is a deliberate and strategic approach by major corporations to trick consumers. As people generally do not like being fooled, this approach positions listeners to view such corporations negatively, and hence be open to Green-Moore's suggestions regarding ethical consumerism.

Green-Moore subsequently changes her approach, returning the focus to individual members of her audience and the actions they can personally take. She continues to depict manufacturers negatively, highlighting their 'nasty tactics' and 'vague response[s]' that indicate they aren't 'being honest'. Green-Moore presents ethical consumerism as a good-versus-evil battle, with huge corporations being on the 'bad' side, and those who wish to shop sustainably as the heroes. This positions the audience as wanting to align themselves with the heroes, and thus encourages them to be receptive to her suggestions of how to make ethical purchases, particularly when they are described as 'easy changes'. While she acknowledges that there will be challenges, such as 'say[ing] goodbye to a much-loved favourite', she emphasises that the actions required to make a difference are 'small', but 'will all add up', reassuring listeners that these are things that they can do without much effort. The idea that the actions of each individual matter is reinforced by the first image from the presentation, which features a hand erasing smoke that is belching out of a chimney. The image depicts a single hand doing the erasing, which suggests that just one person doing something can have a significant impact on the environment. The simplicity of the image and the tools being used – a common eraser – implies that positive action doesn't require complex materials, and is something that anyone can do. Through the combined effects of the implications of the visual and the direct strategies that Green-Moore provides, the suggestion is that the audience have the power to counteract the negative actions of big businesses, if they incorporate ethical consumerism into their daily lives.

To conclude, Green-Moore re-emphasises her friendly, open persona, encouraging listeners to approach her with questions – or even just for a chat – after the presentation has finished. This aims to reinforce that she shares the same goals as the audience, and that 'a more environmentally friendly and sustainable community' is something that can only be achieved by working together. Her closing line is a final call to action, reinforcing the 'us versus them' focus of the presentation, as she challenges her listeners not to 'let the big corporations trick' you. This once again emphasises the negative intentions of the manufacturers by implying that they want to deceive consumers, and also reminds her audience of the need to be alert to their dirty tactics. Having alerted her eco-conscious audience to the strategies being used on them, she encourages them to shop responsibly and mindfully, in order to practise ethical consumerism successfully.

Sample response 3: Highfield Markets

With the Highfield area having become an increasingly desirable place to live, it has been facing changes. One such change, the proposed demolition of the local markets and their replacement with a supermarket, has angered local resident Ravi Nicholson, and he addresses the issue in a podcast episode. Targeting a wide demographic of local residents, with the material being published across a range of platforms and formats, Nicholson condemns the planned redevelopment and urges his fellow residents to actively oppose the proposal.

The podcast opens with Nicholson addressing his listeners in a friendly manner and providing context about the Highfield Markets. The conversational and direct greeting that he begins with suggests that rapport exists between Nicholson and his listeners, and positions him as a trusted voice within the community. He conveys a sense of urgency around the issue from the outset by highlighting that this is an unexpected edition of the podcast, 'a bonus feature' that he 'couldn't sit on … until next week', building a sense of anticipation about what is to follow. Nicholson moves on to discussing the changes that have occurred in the area recently, speaking positively about their contribution to the community. His upbeat comments on 'the new local pool', 'the green spaces' and 'the street veggie patch' depict him as someone who is not opposed to change, and also enable him to position himself as community-focused. All the changes he mentions are examples of areas in Highfield being used for the benefit of the community, which is in direct opposition to the commercial proposal that he subsequently criticises, highlighting to his listeners that the community is his priority. Nicholson also presents himself as someone with a longstanding connection to Highfield, explaining how he has 'been running around those stalls since [he] was five' and that his children do the same now. This has the dual intended impact of emphasising that Nicholson understands what is important to Highfield because of his personal experience as a resident, and also demonstrating the importance of the markets as a community social hub as well as a place to buy things.

After introducing the proposed demolition of the markets in his opening, Nicholson then discusses the planned replacement in scathing terms. Referring to the proposed supermarket in consistently negative language, he positions it as the opposite of everything that the community stands for, using descriptions such as 'just another chain store' and 'another lifeless supermarket'. Nicholson seeks to position Highfield residents to see the existing markets as essential to the community, humanising the markets as providing the community 'with a heartbeat' and referring to several market traders by name. The contrast seeks to emphasise to local listeners that the markets provide many benefits, not just produce, in comparison with the cold, impersonal replacement that is being proposed. This disparity between the existing and the proposed is further emphasised through the visuals included on the website. The initial photograph shows a welcoming scene, with busy stalls in a sunlit, tree-lined park. The market is bustling, and people of different ages are shown interacting and enjoying the stalls. The second photo depicts the complete opposite, with a single person shown among empty, bare market stalls. In contrast to the energy evident in the first image, the second photo is lifeless and cold, implying that the closure of the market will lead to a similar loss of community for Highfield, thus encouraging the audience to support Nicholson in opposing the redevelopment.

Nicholson concludes his podcast episode by reminding his listeners of the need for action, outlining a number of things that they can do to support the markets. He references the 'protest posters and signs' that have already been put up, 'applaud[ing] those who created' them, which adds strength to his position by indicating that others have also been actively advocating for the markets. This presents it as a campaign that is well supported, which may encourage listeners to also get involved, as they feel that there is strength in numbers. Nicholson provides a range of ways that people can support the markets, referring to an online petition, writing to the council and shopping at the markets, thus suggesting that, no matter the age of the listener or the time they have available, there is something that they can do that would help save the markets. His use of multiple imperatives – 'write', 'make', 'head down', 'support' – serve as direct calls to action specifying what readers can do. He softens this somewhat by highlighting the benefits to listeners, reminding them that they will be 'getting some great produce' as well as supporting the markets. Through his direct language, appeal to local interest and suggestion that they would be part of a larger campaign, Nicholson urges his listeners to take action to support the markets and reject the proposed redevelopment.

Sample response 4: Handwriting

Leslie Slater responds to concerns about the increased use of computers and the resulting potential negative effects of decreased use of handwriting in an article published in a school newsletter that is emailed to parents. Primarily addressing parents, Slater contends that handwriting should not be abandoned, due to its role in aiding memory and also its appeal to the senses.

Adopting a conversational tone to gain rapport with the readers, Slater argues that handwriting is an expression of a person's individuality. By describing handwriting using words with positive connotations such as 'personal and unique' and 'an expression of the individual', Slater aims to stimulate in parents a desire for their children to develop handwriting skills in order to be able to express their personality. In the first photograph, the beautiful handwriting created by the fountain pen not only draws readers' attention to the possibility of their children being able to create beautiful and unique handwriting, but also elicits their admiration for handwriting and their desire for their children to express themselves. Slater often uses lyrical and literary language when describing handwriting, such as in the statement 'mirror held up to their human creator', and she dwells on the physical sensations associated with writing by hand. This strategy has the aim of elevating handwriting to an art as well as something inherently meaningful, positioning readers to feel that something valuable would be lost if young people no longer learned to write by hand.

By contrast, Slater juxtaposes handwriting against using computers, which are described in negative terms as 'mechanical' and 'mass-produced', qualities that sound dehumanising and unappealing to parents. Slater supports her analysis by citing Philip Hensher's book *The Missing Ink* to give readers confidence in her opinion, suggesting that it is supported by expert researchers. She also associates handwriting with successful people, in order to reinforce parents' desire for their children to develop good handwriting, since most people want their children to be successful and to have the money to purchase items such as the fountain pen in the photograph, a symbol of wealth and status.

Slater expresses concerns about the decrease in students' opportunities to practise handwriting. Adopting a logical tone of voice, reflected in phrases such as 'typing ... is the vastly more common way in which students produce written work', the writer hopes to elicit the reader's confidence in her opinion, as she appears to be simply stating facts. Their confidence is reinforced by citing the opinion of Kim Jones: parents are likely to believe Jones because she is an 'experienced English and Literature teacher' who would be genuinely concerned about the welfare and academic progress of students such as the readers' children. By stating that some students 'fail' to complete their important Year 12 exams, Slater intends to arouse parental concerns because they will not want their children to be deprived of post-secondary opportunities. Although they may be experts in using a computer keyboard – as depicted in the second photograph, which shows a pair of hands typing with all ten fingers – their handwriting may not be adequate for the exams, as symbolised by the pencil, sitting next to the computer and not being used.

Slater further contends that there is a link between handwriting and brain development. She cites a number of facts — such as that those who wrote by hand 'wrote more and they wrote faster' — from two research projects, the first involving adults and the second involving children, to support this idea and to elicit reader confidence that outcomes are better, at all ages, if people write by hand. In particular, parents are meant to have confidence in the first piece of research because of the expert status of the researcher Virginia Berninger, a 'professor of educational psychology'. Slater's citation of expert testimony appeals to the reader's sense of reason and logic. This balances the more emotive aspects of Slater's argument, thus broadening her argument's relevance to a diverse audience.

By emphasising the positive aspects of handwriting, framing it as 'valuable, unique and often beautiful', Slater encourages parents to feel compelled to support preserving handwriting.

Sample response 5: Penny's Petals

In her blog post entitled 'Shock in the shop! The ethics of cut flowers', florist Penelope Acosta contrasts the mass-produced flower industry, which she depicts as unethical, with her own florist shop. Addressing members of the general public, particularly those who purchase cut flowers, Acosta hopes readers will be disgusted with the cut-flower industry, refuse to buy their flowers, and instead admire and purchase flowers produced by florists such as herself.

Acosta commences her blog post with a personal anecdote about how she became interested in the flower industry. By contrasting the 'beautiful bouquet' of roses with them being produced at the 'wrong time of year' and asking the question, 'How were these flowers in bloom in autumn?', Acosta elicits a sense of curiosity in her readers. The contrast shows a logical contradiction, encouraging readers to continue reading her post to resolve this contradiction. This curiosity is reinforced when she next states that the roses 'had a far more sinister background'. With its negative connotations and associations of evil and harm, the word 'sinister' invites readers to feel a sense of trepidation, which is reinforced through the photo at the start of the post. While the rose in the bottle in the front right of the photo appears to be healthy, symbolic of the beauty and enticing nature of mass-produced flowers, it is contrasted against the wilting rose in the shadow on the left, symbolic of the negative aspects of the flower industry, positioning readers to be concerned about this industry. The contradiction, together with the sombre colours of the photo and the use of shadow, convey a sense of deception and potential danger, likely to alarm the reader.

Acosta then lists the negative facets of the cut-flower industry. The statistics she cites, such as the industry 'being worth an estimated US$55 billion', position readers to realise how huge this industry is and, by implication, its high level of exploitation. Using cause-and-effect logic, Acosta insinuates that the industry exploits workers. For example, they have to work '16-hour days', implying they are overworked and mistreated. She then states that such workers are exposed to 'fertilisers, insecticides and preservatives that are absolutely full of toxins', positioning readers to believe that such products harm the workers and to therefore sympathise with them. This is reinforced by listing the negative effects upon the local communities. By then stating that young children who come in contact with such workers have been assessed for altered short-term brain activity, Acosta implies that these children's physiological health has suffered, eliciting a sense of pity for such children, who are essentially vulnerable victims of these exploitative practices, as well as anger at those who run such operations. Furthermore, by describing such farms as characterised by 'exploitation' and 'unscrupulous' practices, with their negative connotations of unethical behaviour, Acosta suggests that those who run such ventures have no consideration for the welfare of their fellow human beings, thus reinforcing reader sympathy for the workers and disgust at the managers. Therefore, by appealing to the ethical values of the readers, particularly their sense of fair play, she positions those readers who have bought such flowers to feel a sense of guilt, as they are meant to infer that they have contributed to the exploitation of people in developing countries who lack the protection that workers in developed countries such as Australia enjoy.

Appealing to readers' environmental concerns, Acosta then explores the negative environmental effects of cut flowers. Adopting a concerned tone, Acosta cites the huge quantity of water needed to grow the flowers and states that they are 'putting a strain on local resources'. Readers are positioned to be worried about this negative effect and feel a sense of guilt because, as consumers, they contribute to depriving people of essential resources. She then states that the distribution leaves an 'astronomical carbon footprint', hinting that this is due to the amount of fossil fuels used in planes, trucks and other vehicles to transport the flowers. Her question, 'How could I be sure that the flowers I was buying were ethically sourced and sustainably grown?' not only portrays Acosta as a person of moral integrity, but also invites readers to conclude that the cut flowers they buy are not ethically sourced, and they would be acting hypocritically if they were to continue to purchase such flowers.

Acosta then informs readers that her response to the negative effects of the cut flower industry was to establish her own florist shop. In describing her method of growing flowers, she uses a positive tone in contrast with how she has described the flower industry throughout the rest of the piece. For example, she states that her family uses 'only the most eco-friendly and sustainable of products', does not use foam blocks or plastics – which readers know from her previous discussion damage the environment – and she only sources other flowers from farmers who minimise 'the use of water and toxic chemicals'. This ethical language positions readers to admire the environmentally friendly way in which Acosta acts professionally. Appealing to readers' national pride, she states that she has 'the added pleasure of supporting Australian businesses just like mine', positioning readers to want to buy from her, as readers generally wish to support Australian enterprises. Thus, having read this article, Acosta hopes that the readers – motivated by a sense of guilt at contributing to exploitative practices and environmental damage – will not buy imported flowers, but instead – motivated by a sense of patriotism and responsibility to care for the environment – purchase flowers from her business.

Sample response 6: The wearable workplace

In an article entitled 'The wearable workplace', published in the online publication *SuitNoTie*, Brannigan Forsythe discusses the benefits of 'working wearables'. He addresses a readership of business executives, encouraging them to adopt these items in their businesses to improve productivity.

Forsythe begins the article by stating that wearables are already in use. Adopting a positive upbeat tone, reflected in phrases such as 'there's plenty of room for businesses to get in on the action' and 'supercharge their operations', he aims to arouse executives' curiosity as to how wearables could be used by businesses. The positive connotation of the term 'supercharge', with its associations of revitalisation, positions executives to believe that adopting wearables may lead to exponential growth, encouraging them to continue reading to learn how they could implement them in their businesses.

The author then examines three types of wearables. The first of these is fitness trackers. Appealing secondarily to the sense of concern employers should have for their employees, but predominantly to their financial concerns, Forsythe encourages employers to provide employees with items such as Fitbits. By stating that 'fitter and healthier employees have higher energy levels, are less likely to get sick and are more productive in the long term' and 'the cost for the company is relatively small' Forsythe implies that the cost of providing an employee with a Fitbit is less than the losses due to sick leave. Executives who may be reluctant for their companies to purchase such items for employees are thus positioned to purchase them. Furthermore, Forsythe acknowledges the difficulties employers face in ordering employees to care more for their health. However, by suggesting that employers should supply employees with a Fitbit – which he implies should be done as 'the cost for the company is relatively small' – Forsythe suggests that this would motivate employees to monitor their fitness as they are getting a device for free. He suggests this would also give them the message that the company genuinely cares for them, thereby motivating them to be more productive in their work. The final rhetorical question in their section 'what would you prefer to be paying for? A fitness tracker – which is getting cheaper by the day – or the cost of covering sick leave?' underscores the cost-benefit dynamic the writer is arguing, and aims to lead the reader to the desired response of agreement with the writer.

Forsythe then proceeds to explore how exoskeletons and Wearsafe minimise injuries. Continuing to appeal to employers' financial concerns, he describes injuries in retail and manufacturing as 'crippling'. With its negative connotations and associations with the demise of a company, by using this word the writer seeks to instil fear into business executives who would be looking for any reasonable opportunity to avoid compensation payments that would harm their company. While he acknowledges that there is no way to avoid injury entirely, and in so doing makes his argument appear to be more measured and therefore credible, he notes that exoskeletons in Audi have reduced 'the stress on workers' bodies'. This reference to Audi – a reputable car manufacturing company in Germany – is intended to position executives to consider adopting this to reduce their liability. He then discusses Wearsafe, which gives an accurate location of a worker who has been injured. He argues that time is of the essence when responding to an injury, and so introducing this device would help employers feel confident. By describing it as a 'deceptively simple' solution, a common expression that underscores the ease of utility and implementation, Forsythe appeals to executives' sense of convenience.

Forsythe then advocates the benefits of wearing sensors to track mental health. Reminding readers that 'poor mental health is just as much of a drain on productivity as physical injury', Forsythe again appeals to executives' sense of duty of care to their employees, as well as their financial interest. Adopting an excited tone when he says, 'Well, good news, folks! There's a wearable for that', he encourages readers to share his enthusiasm, since they are meant to believe that these devices could easily, and relatively inexpensively, solve reduced productivity as a result of mental health issues. Furthermore, mentioning Hitachi as an early adopter of this scheme bolsters his argument's credibility. In addition, Forsythe appeals to sense of modernity when he states that 'companies all over the world are using similar tech to … determine when [employees] might be in need of a break (or a little more incentive!)', positioning executives to feel a sense of concern if they do not adopt this cutting-edge technology, since their rivals may gain a market advantage with increased productivity.

Forsythe then rebuts the objection that employees may consider such devices – with their data-collecting capabilities – to be a breach of privacy. Adopting a measured tone, Forsythe acknowledges the concerns employees have about the misuse of data. By noting that a survey indicates 82 per cent of people have such concerns and by stating that such data collection 'is likely to be met with some resistance', he reminds executives that an attempt to introduce wearables may be difficult. The cartoon showing an employee reading a text message on his smart watch saying 'You're fired' while he is running reminds executives that this technology could be used in an unethical way, and that this would undermine its benefits. Hence, Forsythe then states that 'the real issue, then, is trust' and that what is needed is a comprehensive plan of education before introducing this technology. In providing this solution to the conundrum of employee resistance, Forsythe attempts to subtly manoeuvre employers into adopting an educational program that will gain workers' support and approval.

In ending his article by saying 'it's clear wearables are here to stay', Forsythe reminds employers that wearables are an integral part of the future of work; hence, they will need to be embraced. By then stating 'keen CEOs need to keep ahead of the curve – or watch the revolution pass them by', Forsythe positions executives to feel concerned that, if they do not embrace wearables, rival companies may outperform their own.

Sample response 7: Halloween

The impending arrival of the end of October has led to a number of Redfern residents expressing their opinion about Halloween and its associated activities in the local newspaper. Nadia Laghari is one such resident, sharing her point of view in an opinion piece printed in the free publication. In a lighthearted and warm manner, she explains how her views of Halloween have evolved, encouraging other Redfern locals, particularly fellow parents, to embrace the celebration as an opportunity for community togetherness.

Laghari begins by outlining her original negative opinion of Halloween, and the reasons why she disliked it. She highlights the existing extensive 'American influence in our culture', appealing to her Australian audience who may be concerned about this, before shifting her attention to the impact on families. She references the many challenges for families that Halloween raises, outlining a 'school night' schedule that would be familiar to many parent readers, with Halloween on top of 'the dinnertime schedule' and 'sports training' resulting in 'havoc'. By presenting herself as a parent who knows the scheduling challenges that families face, she seeks to build rapport with readers who are also parents, in order to then demonstrate that they could undergo a similar change of mind to hers. Laghari also highlights the negatives of Halloween from a health and environmental perspective, emphasising how there is 'so much waste', and describing it as a 'sugary occasion' based 'on the mass consumption of lollies'. This positions her as a socially conscious writer, who cares not only about her own children, but about the wider impact of celebrations on the environment. Laghari's depiction of Halloween as sugar-focused is supported by the first image she includes, which is a photograph of an array of lollies spilling out of a plastic bucket. The lollies dominate the photo, implying that the entire focus of the event is on mass-produced sugary treats, and the inclusion of the 'plastic-wrapped candy' and plastic bucket also emphasises the negative environmental impact of the event. Through a variety of visual and written language devices, Laghari positions readers, especially parents, to acknowledge the negative aspects of Halloween celebrations.

Having established the reasons for her previous disapproval of Halloween, Laghari explains what prompted her change of opinion. In contrast to the negativity of the previous paragraph, she emphasises the joy that she now finds in the celebrations, focusing on the opportunities for community interaction. Through repeated reference to connection – 'kids… with their friends', 'say[ing] hello to neighbours', 'meet[ing] the new families' – Laghari encourages her audience of fellow Redfern residents to see Halloween as an opportunity for building connection with others in the local area. Through this, new residents are positioned to feel welcome, and longer-term inhabitants are reminded of the importance of community spirit. This emphasis on the neighbourhood is also evident in her suggestions regarding alternatives to lollies, as she contrasts the commercial and impersonal 'plastic-wrapped candy' with 'home-baked cookies and fruit from the community garden', suggesting that even the treats that are shared on Halloween can be an opportunity for family or community connection. Having initially presented Halloween negatively as a foreign celebration based on excess, Laghari repositions it as an opportunity to connect with fellow residents, thus encouraging local Redfern readers to use the evening to build relationships with others in the community.

Continuing her focus on connection, Laghari narrows her discussion to highlight the opportunities Halloween provides for family interaction. She repeats her concerns about the wastefulness of Halloween, with costumes 'thrown away 24 hours later', reinforcing her position as environmentally, as well as socially, conscious, before going on to discuss her alternative approach. Laghari makes repeated use of positively connoted words – 'imaginatively', 'creative', 'opportunity' 'inspired' – presenting the activity of costume creation as something that is not only environmentally beneficial but also enriching and stimulating for both herself and her children. Parents in the audience are positioned to see Halloween as a chance to 'impart some lessons' to their children, in a way that is practical and enjoyable. This is further reinforced by the article's second photograph, which features three smiling children in Halloween costumes. While lollies do still feature in this image, they are simply one component of it, rather than the focus. Here, the focus is on the smiling faces of the children, conveying happiness and enjoyment, positioning Redfern parents to see Halloween as a positive event. The costumes are simple, connecting to Laghari's suggestion of 'reusing and recycling', and the jack-o'-lanterns in this photo are real, implying that they have been created as a family activity. Laghari's message of sustainability and family connection is highlighted through both the visual and written language, encouraging readers to embrace the positive opportunities provided by Halloween.

To conclude, Laghari reinforces her own change of opinion, and highlights the opportunity that Halloween offers the community. By acknowledging that she 'used to push back against' Halloween, she reminds readers that changing one's mind is acceptable, encouraging them to share her newfound positive view of the celebrations. She positions Halloween in a wider context, highlighting that most major celebrations in Australia are imported, thus providing justification for enjoying a traditionally American event. Through her emphasising of the 'unique' nature of Australia, Laghari positions readers to embrace Halloween celebrations, and to view them as an opportunity to bring people together for 'a community catch-up'.

Sample response 8: The Salty Boot

Local residents want a local music venue, The Salty Boot, to be closed primarily because of loud noise. This has led to a rally in support of keeping it open. At this protest, middle-aged rock musician Vince D'Angelo gives a speech. Addressing fans of The Salty Boot, D'Angelo outlines why he thinks it should remain open.

D'Angelo begins his speech by reminding his listeners that The Salty Boot will soon close. In a nostalgic tone, he says he has a 'heavy heart.' This phrase, with negative connotation of sadness, invites listeners to share his regret at the imminent closure. In this first section of the speech, D'Angelo also identifies the reason The Salty Boot is closing – residents' complaints – to provoke listeners' contempt for people complaining. By describing the neighbourhood as 'gentrified' D'Angelo suggests that wealthy new residents believe that they – because of their social status – have the right to decide which venues close. D'Angelo invites listeners to feel mad at these people. Listeners' contempt for these residents is mean to be reinforced by D'Angelo's description of them as 'complainers', a word that implies they are negative and their complaints are not valid. The statistic that more than 80 per cent of Melbourne residents want The Salty Boot to stay open positions readers to be further angered by the local residents – since a small minority appear to be succeeding in getting what they want.

In his argument that The Salty Boot should remain open, D'Angelo then reflects on its significance in his life and the lives of his listeners. By calling The Salty Boot a 'home', D'Angelo wants listeners to believe that the venue is a comfortable, warm, inviting and happy place, as a home should be. By listing some of his own experiences of the venue – for example, it was the first place he heard live rock-and-roll, and the place where he ordered his first beer – he positions listeners to share his nostalgic feelings, as they probably have had many similar experiences. D'Angelo then discusses the critical role The Salty Boot has played in supporting emerging artists. By naming himself, as well as Trombone Jackson, who he says is an 'internationally acclaimed musician', D'Angelo wants readers to share his admiration for the venue for supporting such musicians. Relying on cause-and-effect logic, he wants readers to believe that The Salty Boot was essential to their success.

D'Angelo then identifies other negative effects of the closure on the lives of his listeners at the rally. In a series of statements, each beginning with the phrase 'say goodbye to the Boot', he lists these effects: for example, 'Say goodbye to the Boot and we're three-quarters of the way to boring.' As nobody would want to live a boring life, with its associations of meaninglessness and lack of activity, D'Angelo hopes fellow supporters of The Salty Boot will be concerned about the negative impact on their emotional wellbeing. Reinforcing his cause-and-effect argument about The Salty Boot being important to musicians' success, he wants listeners to be alarmed at the prospect that the closure could mean future musicians will not be discovered.

D'Angelo then returns to criticism of the local residents. By contrasting their attitude when they were young supporters of The Salty Boot – who 'drank and screamed and danced all night' – with their current opposition, D'Angelo suggests that local residents of his own generation opposing the closure are hypocrites, inviting the listeners to share his contempt for them. This contempt is reinforced by D'Angelo labelling the neighbourhood 'gentrified', with its associations of being exclusionary, classist and lacking in diversity. The listeners are meant to feel pity for the residents' children when D'Angelo asks, 'but let these kids do the same? Absolutely not', implying they over-protect their children by not allowing them to have experiences associated with entering adulthood such as going to The Salty Boot. Adopting a sarcastic tone, D'Angelo states that the only creativity their children 'can appreciate is latte art.' This is a skill practised by baristas in 'gentrified' cafes; hence, D'Angelo suggests that children's creative aspirations and skills will be restricted by their parents, positioning readers to dismiss opponents' objections to The Salty Boot. The cartoon in the leaflet advertising the rally depicts a similarly negative image of local residents. Sandwiched between two high-rise apartment blocks in the cartoon's foreground, The Salty Boot is portrayed by Roisin McCrae as being squeezed out by the residents, and being intimidated by them, positioning readers to feel anger towards the residents. Readers are also meant to be outraged by the depictions of residents' aggressive and rude behaviours in the cartoon – such as grabbing a guitar off a young man, yelling and shaking their fists – because people expect others to be polite and civil. Ending the speech in a defiant tone, seen in the phrase 'Well folks, I for one am not going to let them destroy this place', D'Angelo encourages listeners to stand together and actively oppose the closure.

Sample response 9: Golf course development

In response to the need to redevelop the Westhaven Showgrounds, Alejandra Ortega from Ortega Landscape Design gives a speech in which she contends that the dilapidated site should be converted into a golf course. She addresses local residents, many of whom may oppose the redevelopment.

Ortega begins her presentation by stating that she was raised in Westhaven. Delivered in an excited tone, statements such as 'I'm a local Westhaven girl through and through' are meant to establish rapport with her audience, who are positioned to perceive her as being genuinely interested in the needs of the local community. For the same reason, later in the speech, Ortega acknowledges the concerns of some residents. She then outlines the positive aspects of golf. Firstly, she states that it is growing in popularity. By citing a figure – '250 000 more Australians played golf than in the previous year' – Ortega emphasises this popularity, encouraging others to want to be a part of this trend, and also presents herself as having an in-depth knowledge of the business side of golf, which inclines listeners to trust her. In addition, local residents are encouraged to have a positive attitude towards golf, and thus be more open to her proposal to redevelop the Showgrounds. Using a series of questions that appeal to listeners' desires to increase their fitness and socialise with others, such as 'Seeking a gentle form of aerobic exercise? Golf!', Ortega then invites the audience to consider how golf could benefit them.

Ortega then contrasts the benefits of golf with the current substandard state of the Showgrounds. By stating that the use of the facilities for community events 'such as parties, school events and weddings' has declined 'by over 40% in the last four years', Ortega not only validates her observation that 'the community is not making use of the facilities' but also implies that council revenue from such events has decreased. Listeners are meant to infer that this is one reason 'the council cannot afford to maintain' the Showgrounds. Ortega then describes the poor state of the current facilities. Through her use of the words 'rusting grandstand, dilapidated fencing and old toilet block', with their associations of age and decay, local residents are positioned to believe that a significant amount of money needs to be spent on repairs and ongoing maintenance, which cannot be justified given the fact that the facilities are underused. She subtly appeals to residents' financial interest, as they are meant to infer that this shortfall will need to be paid for by the council from the rates residents pay. This negative description is complemented by a photograph of the grandstand. Not only do the facilities look out of date, but the signs of deterioration – for example, the flaking paint – position listeners to feel disdain for these facilities and believe that urgent rectification is needed, and thus to feel more open to the golf course proposal.

Ortega then contrasts the current facilities with the proposed golf course. Adopting an enthusiastic tone, she appeals to local residents' civic pride when she states, 'we all want to have pride in our local environment'. Furthermore, by describing Westhaven using words with positive connotations of good fortune and growth – 'we have a beautiful and vibrant town' – Ortega positions local residents to feel confident that this proposal will enhance the local community. In this section of the speech, Ortega also appeals to listeners' desires for facilities that will benefit them, for example, 'it will give residents the opportunity to nurture or begin a passion for golf without having to travel away from Westhaven'. The picture shown to listeners at this point in the presentation, which contrasts with that of the grandstand, shows two children playing golf. The open space and sunlight add to the positive impression of this picture and reinforce listeners' excitement about the proposal, as they are encouraged to imagine their own families participating in a fun, wholesome activity. Ortega also appeals to listeners' financial self-interest. By stating that 'as private developers, we have a significant budget', she implies that the developers, and not the local community, will be paying for the costs of the redevelopment. In addition, by stating that it will 'bring much-needed tourist dollars', Ortega elicits listeners' enthusiasm for the project as she suggests that revenue from tourists, not local residents, will largely pay for the ongoing maintenance.

In the final section of the speech, Ortega allays listeners' concerns about losing access to this community space. She states that 'the project is not designed to alienate anyone', thus appealing to her listeners' need for a sense of belonging. She again underscores how the redevelopment will benefit residents, listing various features such as the restaurant, running track and mini-golf course for children. Residents are positioned to feel relieved, and also excited at the prospect of enjoying 'fresh air and exercise in beautiful, well-kept parklands'. She concludes her speech by inviting residents to approach her with questions or concerns, again presenting herself as having genuine empathy and willingness to discuss valid concerns listeners may have, reinforcing rapport with her audience and positioning them to believe that she wants to address their concerns.

Sample response 10: Fast fashion

In a blog post, Alessandra DuBois, owner of a second-hand clothing store, contends that people should stop purchasing fast fashion and instead support more sustainable clothing practices. She hopes her customers will encourage acquaintances who consume 'fast fashion' to read this post.

DuBois begins her post with a call for readers to consider carefully their spending habits in relation to fashion. The picture before the text introduces the main ideas in the article. The woman wearing a fashionable outfit and carrying a number of shopping bags represents the person 'who buys on-trend outfits' but does not recognise the 'impact' of their shopping habits, a description designed to elicit a sense of guilt in readers who engage in similar purchasing habits. This guilt is reinforced by the image of a tip with huge piles of rubbish, which suggests to readers who purchase fast fashion that their selfish actions have resulted in excessive landfill. At the end of this introductory description, DuBois gives an urgent call to action, asking readers to forward this post to those who purchase fast fashion. Presenting the statement 'This is their intervention' in bold letters emphasises the seriousness of the issue and aims to evoke alarm in the reader. In doing this, DuBois hopes readers will be shocked and shamed by her post and so will be inclined to adopt the alternative practices she recommends.

Fast fashion is described in negative terms throughout the post. The phrase 'toxic culture', with its connotations of damage and even death, alludes to the harm DuBois claims it causes to both the environment and workers. Readers are meant to be shocked at such negative effects and feel a sense of guilt that their behaviour has contributed to it. DuBois supports and validates her condemnation of the fast-fashion industry in readers' minds by using facts and figures to convey the extent of the harm it causes. For example, it uses 93 billion cubic metres of water – an amount readers are meant to believe is excessive. Furthermore, the wastewater dumped into rivers is described as 'toxic', repeating the emotive word and emphasising its negative connotations by specifying that it contains 'substances such as lead, mercury and arsenic'. Readers who are aware of how dangerous these chemicals are to 'both wildlife and humans' are meant to be horrified about their harmful effects, reinforcing their sense of guilt because they are contributing to this damage through purchasing fast fashion. DuBois then identifies the excessive carbon footprint – '26% of our total' – should these trends continue, implying that alternative courses of action need to be pursued immediately, particularly given the 'urgency of the issue'. The use of figures also suggests to readers that DuBois is knowledgeable and that her opinion is based on research, giving it greater credibility.

DuBois then outlines the negative effects of the fast-fashion industry on humans. Appealing to readers' moral values and their empathy for others, she outlines the negative impact on workers, who are forced to endure 'unbearably long hours for terribly low pay' in 'extremely hazardous working conditions'. Use of the words 'unbearably' and 'extremely' aims to intensify the readers' sympathy, positioning them to reject fast fashion out of a desire not to be associated with such suffering. This description is followed by the rhetorical question, 'Given all this, how can anyone consciously continue to support fast fashion?', which encourages readers to consider the alternatives DuBois proceeds to outline, such as her shop.

Next, DuBois outlines the qualities of sustainable clothing, directly contrasting them with fast fashion to emphasise their superiority. By stating that the products are 'sustainably sourced' and 'made from durable materials', she positions readers to admire and desire these products. She also subtly appeals to readers' financial interest, since they will not be wasting money on shoddy garments. Readers are also meant to feel a sense of pride should they adopt DuBois' subtle suggestion to donate their unwanted clothes to a thrift store. In addition, she states that many companies also source clothing that uses 'eco-friendly manufacturing and fair labour', implying that ethical alternatives to fast fashion are easily accessible. Readers are meant to admire such alternatives and believe that it is their moral duty to buy such clothing instead of continuing to purchase items that cause environmental problems and exploit vulnerable people. The photograph shows an image of a sustainable fashion label that lists the positive qualities of sustainable clothing mentioned in the article (for example, 'Respect Workers' and 'Care for the Earth'), which reinforces readers' admiration for these products and evokes a sense of duty to buy them. DuBois ends the article with a call to action, 'So, get out there and spread the message: the era of fast fashion is dead', implying that readers will inevitably have adopted her point of view after following her ethically based reasoning.

Sample response 11: Sunflower plantations

The sharp increase in tourists taking photos of the sunflower fields of Sunnyside led to sunflower farmer Harvey Sunshine addressing an emergency local council meeting to propose charging tourists a fee to take photos. The image accompanying his speech establishes him as a concerned farmer, and his speech targets the wider community, aiming to appeal to their pride in their town and their feelings of protectiveness for it. He also targets their economic self-interest and develops a strongly negative image of tourists, aimed at evoking listeners' anger.

Sunshine uses his position as a well-known local and a man of action to draw listeners to his side. He uses casual and inclusive language to address the audience as friends, 'fellow farmers' who have 'come to know' him over the years. He uses humour and self-mockery (describing himself as the 'resident curmudgeon') to put the audience at ease, to encourage them to listen to and support his views. He also acknowledges his 'reputation' as someone who often complains, in order to set his concern about this issue apart from his previous complaints, because 'every now and then, axes need grinding'. The phrase 'every now and then' suggests that this only applies to issues of particular importance, setting the listeners up to feel that the damage being done by tourists is severe and worthy of their attention. He directs the meeting to do something about the tourist problem with an inclusive call for support – 'we must speak our mind, loudly and clearly' – that positions locals to share his view that this is about a serious problem needing immediate action. This phrase also frames the issue as connected to self-expression and the right of everyone in the room to voice their opinion, an idea most listeners would support.

Sunshine shifts his focus to the 'huge increase in the number of tourists' and the damage they are causing for locals, while blaming the council for inaction. The photograph of him looking carefully at a bent flower head with the caption 'Harvey Sunshine inspects his sunflowers for damage' illustrates his claim that the number of tourists is 'causing havoc' and damaging crops. The care with which he examines the flowers supports his claim to be concerned about them and helps to present him as gentle and well-intentioned. The fact that he is not looking at the camera and that he is alone, together with the soft lighting, also helps to convey a sense of vulnerability that is likely to arouse feelings of protectiveness in listeners.

In contrast to this kindly depiction of himself and farmers like him, Sunshine uses colourful language to create a sense of urgency about the situation and to present the tourists as warlike invaders arriving in 'hordes', 'armed to the teeth', 'scaling [his] fence, or cutting the wire'. These phrases have connotations of destruction and invasion, encouraging the audience to think that the behaviour of the tourists is out of control and needs to be managed, and to feel that their town is under siege from a serious 'enemy'. The threat extends even to his animals and grandchildren, a situation likely to arouse listeners' concern and sympathy, as well as fear for their own families and homes.

Sunshine follows with an appeal to reason about the financial cost for farmers by using personal anecdotes of careless visitors trampling 'hundreds of dollars of plants underfoot' and 'snap[ping] off the heads' of his plants as souvenirs, in an appeal to residents' financial self-interest that aims to lead other locals to agree that such behaviour cannot be ignored and that costs need to be covered. Thus he presents the careless visitors as causing harm on many levels, creating a highly negative picture of them that feeds into the 'us and them' dichotomy he builds up throughout his speech.

By labelling the inaction of the local council as 'cowardice', Sunshine aims to arouse scorn in members of the public and shame in council members, thus leading the meeting to support his economic solution of charging tourists to enter properties to take photos. He appeals for support by outlining the potential benefits to the wider business community through associated economic activities like 'coffee carts' and 'markets'. He drives home the need for 'urgent' action by creating a sense of rivalry with another town already charging tourists. The members at the meeting are led to think that, if they don't make the tourists pay, this rival town will gain an economic advantage. By presenting the meeting with a choice between paying for tourist damage themselves or charging the visitors, Sunshine positions the audience to follow the economically rational path of charging for photos. He makes a direct appeal to the meeting with his final repeated calls for 'support'. He uses a progression of pronouns from 'I' to 'you' and 'our' to show that the proposal will benefit more than a few individuals, aiming to make those in the meeting see that it will benefit the whole town. Overall, Sunshine presents himself as a farmer under siege and the issue in terms of the economic cost versus opportunities for the local town.

Sample response 12: Video games in the English classroom

In a speech at a state conference for English teachers, experienced English teacher Margaret Lee contends that teachers should introduce video games into their classrooms. Addressing an audience of English teachers whose initial attitude towards video games is negative, Lee argues that such games lead to improved academic outcomes.

Lee commences by acknowledging teachers' reservations about the academic benefits of video games. For example, she states that they 'might never have thought of video games as a learning tool'. In doing so, Lee suggests that she understands their concerns, helping to establish rapport with her colleagues. Lee establishes a dichotomy between past and current video games. By describing past video games in negative terms (e.g. 'violent' and 'repetitive') Lee suggests that English teachers' negative perceptions of games are out of date. Hence, listeners are meant to infer that their belief that such games lead to 'aggression and laziness' is a biased and shallow dismissal of the benefits of video games that is not founded on a realistic assessment of the current reality. By repeatedly stating that the era of such games is 'long gone', Lee underscores her assertion that simplistic and shallow video games are a thing of the past. This is intended to elicit a sense of guilt from teachers inclined to dismiss outright the benefits of video games.

Lee then contrasts the deficiencies of earlier video games with the positive attributes of current games. Adopting a confident tone, and by using terms with positive connotations to describe the new games such as 'sophisticated', 'engaging storylines' and 'stunning animation', she attempts to elicit English teachers' admiration for these games. The first image, which portrays a man and a horse in a wilderness area, is an example of the 'stunning animation' in contemporary video games to which Lee refers throughout her speech. This screenshot evokes a rich, vast world to be explored and suggests an imaginative setting, reinforcing her argument that video games are sophisticated texts. Hence, teachers are positioned to believe that such texts would not only engage students but help them to visualise the historical settings of the video games, thereby deepening their learning. Furthermore, by citing her own experience of including video games in English courses 'with great success', Lee positions teachers to be confident about this new proposal. She also encourages English teachers to believe that video games are authentic texts by identifying textual elements such as narrative structure and characters. By stating that players are meant to empathise with characters 'who are very different from themselves', Lee also implies that video games develop students' abilities to interpret characters' attributes, since being able to recognise these facets of people different from themselves is a higher-order cognitive skill. Therefore, by positioning teachers to believe that video games are authentic texts, Lee hopes teachers will support her call for their introduction.

Lee also asserts that playing video games leads to improvement in academic performance. By establishing this cause-and-effect relationship, and by subtly appealing to teachers' desire to be credited with the academic development of their students – particularly through posing the rhetorical question, 'Once they learn those tools, don't you think those students will feel a bit more confident about picking up that novel again?' – Lee positions teachers to support the introduction of video games into their classrooms. Lee reinforces this relationship by citing research by cognitive scientists. The phrase 'cognitive scientists' suggests that Lee's arguments are supported by knowledgable and respected people, further eliciting the trust of teachers. In addition, teachers' belief in the benefits of video games is reinforced by Lee's reference to the impact of video games on improving decision-making (a key cognitive skill) and coordination. By contrasting this benefit against reading a novel, Lee challenges English teachers' beliefs in the superiority of studying texts, implying that video games can have greater academic benefits than the teachers realise.

Lee also supports her argument by citing her own experience as an English teacher. By discussing her initial reluctance to incorporate video games into the classroom, Lee aims to reinforce the rapport established with her colleagues who may have a similar hesitation. By stating 'I considered my students', Lee underscores that her concern is for her students, therefore enhancing her likability. Lee suggests that having developed analytical skills through video games, students will return to reading texts. She hopes teachers will likewise consider the needs of their students and be eager to introduce video games into their classes.

Accompanying the speech is a photograph of young students in a classroom looking eagerly at games on computer screens. Their smiling faces suggest they are engaged in their learning. Teachers are thus meant to have confidence that video games are authentic learning tools that engage students. Lee ends her speech with the declaration that 'it would be a shame to leave these rich texts unexplored when we have them right at our fingertips', which positions English teachers who are still reluctant to introduce video games to feel guilt because they may be depriving their students of an opportunity to experience works of art that they will find genuinely engaging.

Sample response 13: Keeping cats indoors

In an article published in *The Conversation*, a group of professors and academics, including Jaana Dielenberg, Brett Murphy and Chris Dickman, list the dangers both feral and domestic cats pose to the environment. They support their analysis with extensive reference to data and evidence, while using short subheadings to clearly signal their main points of argument for the non-academic reader. Addressing the general public, particularly cat-owners, and adopting a concerned tone, they contend that domestic cats should be kept indoors by their owners.

The writers commence by reminding readers of the number of native animals feral cats kill – over three billion per year – in order to evoke shock and dismay. By then stating 'pet cats are wreaking havoc too', the writers position readers who own a pet cat to feel a sense of concern that their pet may be contributing to the problem. The negatively connotated phrase 'wreaking havoc', with its associations of harmful destruction, paints a negative image in the readers' minds of pets that they consider to be harmless. The impact, which the writers describe as 'staggering', of each pet cat killing '186 reptiles, birds and mammals per year' is cited to elicit a sense of worry among readers. This data reinforces the description of the domestic cat in the article's heading as 'a killing machine'. This phrase implies that cats are serial killers whose behaviour is largely unchecked, thus positioning readers to feel a sense of alarm and a desire to stem the harm cats are causing. In addition, the photograph included with the text, of a domestic cat in the process of killing a native bird, challenges readers' beliefs that their pet is harmless. By portraying the 'killing machine' in action, the writers position readers to feel instead a sense of guilt about the harm caused by their pet.

The writers support their analysis by extensive references to data. By stating that their analysis 'compiles the results of 66 different studies to gauge the impact of Australia's pet cat population on the country's wildlife', they position readers to place an extremely high level of trust in the analysis, since readers are expected to believe that the writers have analysed a large amount of data rather than simply validating their opinions with a selective use of evidence.

The writers then seek to challenge the readers' naive belief that their pet cat is not contributing to the problem. Adopting a concerned tone when they contrast the cat owners' belief that 'their animals don't hunt because they never come across evidence of killed animals' with the reality that 'many pet cats kill animals without bringing them home' encourages readers to question whether their cat has killed native animals. Reader doubt is meant to be reinforced by the reference to the cat video tracking collars and scat analysis, together with the mention that pet cats only bring 15% of their prey home. Readers who believe that their cat does not hunt native animals are pushed to recognise the error of their belief. Cat owners are also expected to generalise the selective video camera and scat tests to their own situation, and infer that their pet cat contributes to the '390 million animals per year in Australia' killed by domestic cats. The writers then rebut cat owners' beliefs that an individual domestic cat has little impact by identifying them as the cause of 'complete losses of populations of some native animal species in their area', eliciting a sense of guilt among owners, who are encouraged to feel a sense of responsibility for protecting native fauna. The writers then challenge readers' assumptions that feral cats are more destructive than domestic cats. They demonstrate – by citing the data – that while an individual feral cat roams a greater distance and kills more animals, given the density of domestic cat populations, with 40 to 70 per square kilometre, pet cats are far more destructive. This is designed to compel readers to feel a sense of guilt at the fact that their negligence has enabled cats to destroy wildlife, and thus to motivate them to be more proactive in preventing their pet from killing native fauna.

The writers conclude the article by arguing that the only solution is for owners to keep their cats indoors. By stating that good diets and bells have limited effects in preventing domestic cats from hunting, the writers hope readers will believe that these solutions are ineffective. Using cause-and-effect logic, the writers also appeal to the readers' self-interest by arguing that keeping cats indoors (cause) prevents various negative outcomes (effect). For example, by stating that cats kept indoors have lower rates of disease which can result in 'illness, miscarriages and birth defects' if transmitted to humans, the writers appeal to the readers' sense of safety, as they are meant to be alarmed at the possibility of a negative medical outcome caused by their pet cat. By stating that 'Australia is in a very good position to make change' and citing public awareness of the problems caused by domestic cats, the writers encourage cat owners to feel a sense of confidence in the positive outcomes that will result from keeping pets indoors.

Sample response 14: Tax on red meat

Local newspaper columnist Parminder Preciosa has written an opinion piece firmly asserting that a tax should be introduced on red meat. Employing informal language and a passionate tone, Preciosa targets readers of her column, particularly those who eat meat, arguing that it is both harmful to people's health and to the environment.

Preciosa commences her article with an extended imaginary scenario as she introduces a familiar situation to her readers. She makes extensive use of positive language such as 'favourite ... restaurant' and 'the moment you've been waiting for' to paint a picture of being about to experience an enjoyable dinner, but the language suddenly becomes negative when she highlights the impact that smoking has on your enjoyment. Verbs such as 'stinging' and 'overpowering' position readers to feel the pain and disgust caused by the cigarette smoke, before she emphasises the likely emotional reaction – 'mad ... furious'. By using the second-person 'you' to present this scenario, she directly places readers in the scene, encouraging them to identify strongly with the negative emotions she describes. They are therefore positioned to feel that, like smoking, meat-eating is distasteful, unpleasant and even anti-social.

After her use of emotional language in the opening of her article, Preciosa then takes a more factual approach by providing evidence of the dangers of smoking, highlighting 'the cost of their [smokers'] habit, both to our society and to themselves' and the 'gruesome medical conditions that can befall even the most casual puffer'. Without yet mentioning a tax on red meat, Preciosa focuses on creating an image of an enjoyable occasion ruined by the selfish behaviour of people consuming a substance that has a significant cost to others. She goes on to suggest that the behaviour of people who eat red meat is similar to the behaviour of smokers, positioning readers to view meat-eaters in a similarly negative light.

Having highlighted the dangers of smoking, Preciosa makes connections between cigarettes and red meat, suggesting that sausages are 'just as much of a threat to your health as that packet of cigs'. She supports this with evidence from the respected global association the World Health Organization, which 'classifies red meat as a carcinogen', and from scientific publications *BMJ Global Health Journal* and *Proceedings of the National Academy of Sciences.* References to such reputable sources implies to readers that Preciosa's view is widely supported and that she has thoroughly researched her argument, thus positioning them to trust in her conclusions. The large numbers of deaths she refers to either as a direct or an indirect result of eating meat are intended to shock the reader into changing their own eating habits out of self-protection and to support a meat tax for the health of others and the planet.

Readers are likely to be familiar with the use of such language and statistics in regard to smoking, but may consider red meat to be a harmless food source. Preciosa acknowledges this potential confusion in her readers, with the comment that foods such as 'bacon and eggs' are 'so delicious', but then highlights that this is 'what they said about cigarettes once upon a time'. By making a further connection between red meat and smoking, Preciosa asserts that readers need to change their views on eating meat, just like society more generally has changed its view on smoking. Her encouragement to readers to question their view of red meat is further enhanced by the photograph that accompanies the article. In it, raw meat appears on a plate in the shape of a question mark. By presenting red meat in this way, readers are invited to question their choices, and to consider whether their enjoyment of red meat is worth the potential negative consequences. The fact that the meat is raw and therefore not fit to eat underscores the point she is making about the undesirability of eating red meat and aims to arouse the reader's disgust.

At this point, having primed the reader to feel negatively towards meat consumption, Preciosa finally states her contention, declaring that a tax on red meat should be introduced. She emphasises the positive economic and health benefits she believes this would have, before highlighting the positive environmental effects of such a tax. She uses these three types of benefits to emphasise the importance of a tax on red meat, and to appeal to a wide range of readers, as it is likely that at least one aspect – economic, health or environmental – will resonate with most readers. Preciosa further explains the environmental impact of meat production, highlighting the '7000 litres of water' needed to produce just '500 grams of beef', which readers may view as wasteful and inefficient, particularly in a naturally dry country such as Australia. She then concludes by reasserting her opinion that a tax on red meat should be introduced by making a final connection between smoking and eating red meat and the societal damage of both. Preciosa attempts to appear balanced by stating that no one should 'dictate what people can and can't do', while attempting to position readers to agree that red meat causes widespread damage and, like cigarettes, it should therefore be taxed.

Sample response 15: Coffee pods

In the opinion piece 'What our love affair with coffee pods reveals about our values' that appeared on *The Conversation* website, writers John Rice and Nigel Martin use a wry, critical tone to contend that Australians' use of coffee pods has skewed our principles. To highlight their point that Australians love the convenience of coffee pods despite environmental issues, the authors open with a photo of a pile of used and discarded coffee pods which need recycling, along with a worrying caption – 'A quick shot, but then what?'. This is followed by the information that most pods 'end up in the bin'. The photo and caption provoke a sense of shame and concern in the reader that not enough is being done to recycle more of these 'convenient' pods. The question in the caption is designed to create uneasiness in the reader about the future of not recycling pods and also serves to raise awareness of the enormity of the problem. As well, the authors' clever use of 'pangs of guilt', 'only tweaked' and the very ugly phrase 'dank pods' is intended to disgust the reader by emphasising the disgraceful fact that many users are happy to ignore the need to recycle pods 'secreted' in a coffee machine, until they have to be disposed of in some way.

Moreover, this evoking of disgust is reinforced by the argument that coffee pod coffee is 'watery, musty and underwhelming', and that the size of the pods was chosen in spite of the negative effect on taste. This argument aims to appeal to readers' self-interest, as many might be deterred by the highly negative description of coffee pods' taste even if they are not moved by the environmental arguments. Furthermore the taste argument reinforces the image of greedy manufacturers who are unconcerned about either the environment or consumers, positioning readers to want to reject their offerings.

In addition, the authors point out that coffee pods are indicative of a 'wider' social problem where the theory of being 'green' is not supported in practice. They use sarcasm in the form of a vivid metaphor, with associations of death and damage, when they describe the coffee industry as being 'as sustainable as an ageing Soviet nuclear power plant' in order to create alarm in the reader at the dangers of not recycling pods – the problems will continue forever. The repetition of 'aluminium' and 'plastic' to describe the pods and the statistics '28 million kilograms of aluminium … sitting in landfill' strongly reinforces for the reader the disastrous effects of theory versus practice. In using 'environmental tsunami' the authors' main aim is to scare readers into recognising the dangers inherent in not recycling pods by suggesting that the amount of waste is unmanageable and even dangerous. On top of this, repetition of the phrase 'environmental problems' reinforces for the reader the sheer wastefulness of throwing out pods and emphasises the importance of practicing 'green' principles.

Furthermore, the authors draw attention to the fact that consumers ignore all criticism of the coffee industry – including 'sourcing practices' which they claim are often 'self-serving'. They use this word to evoke a picture of callous and greedy 'multinational' companies, framing them as deliberately deceptive and self-interested and encouraging readers to consider whether they should trust the companies' business practices. This negative characterisation of coffee pod manufacturers is sustained throughout the piece and extends to the pods themselves, for instance in the sentence 'the march of the pods continues', which implies the pods have a will of their own, a suggestion designed to reinforce the sheer scale of pod proliferation and invoke fear in the reader.

The authors establish that consumers are 'generally supportive of the environment – so long as they don't have to do anything about it'. The article presents a cynical view of consumer behaviour and leaves the reader with a feeling of hopelessness about the future of the environment. This emotional manipulation encourages readers to share the authors' pessimistic view of pod use.

The opinion piece ends on a bleak note, with the authors envisaging 'a less than rosy' future for the environment. For this they blame big businesses who they assert are likely to create more environmental problems rather than solve them. But they also return to their main theme of hypocritical consumers who value 'convenience' over all other considerations. The reader is likely to feel attacked by such direct and blunt criticism, positioning them to want to distance themselves from accusations of selfishness and hypocrisy, support the writers' condemnation of coffee pods and possibly even change their own behaviours.

Sample response 16: Children and screen time

Wattletree Primary School's weekly newsletter contains an open letter to all parents titled 'What Steve Jobs taught me about parenting', by Asif Abdul, a parent himself of two students at the school. He maintains that parents should better monitor their children's screen time, particularly after his discovery that 'Apple founder Steve Jobs limited his children's screen time'. The use of this prominent name in the headline and as a central trigger for writing his letter aims to immediately engage his readers as they are likely to be intrigued about Jobs' input on parenting as he is known more for being a technological innovator, and also keen to learn from someone who has been so successful.

Abdul's repetition of 'I've been thinking' and his query 'why don't I monitor my children's use?' are likely to prompt uneasiness in parents about their own parenting and lead them to begin thinking about their own children's screen time. When he points out the fact that other 'CEOs of tech companies', experts in their field, feel the same as Jobs – also a 'technological guru' – Abdul drives home the point and alarm bells begin to ring for parents as they are set up to question why Jobs limited his own children's screen time.

The phrase 'one of *those* mornings' is meant to disarm his audience, inviting parents to share the common experience of settling a fractious child by using screen time. In this way, Abdul communicates that he understands why parents might turn to screens to soothe children, thus relieving some of the guilt readers might feel and preparing them to heed his message. Having demonstrated this empathy for his audience, Abdul goes on with 'the degree to which we're reliant', and 'for me, and … many others … devices … have become an integral part of parenting', positioning parents to feel uncomfortable about the fact that Jobs and other tech gurus limit screen time and therefore likely to ask themselves more forcefully why it is they rely on 'screens to keep … kids quiet'.

Apart from querying the tech gurus' decisions, Abdul produces as fact that 'many doctors', including neuroscientist Susan Greenfield and US Professor Gary Small, as well as the 'American Academy of Pediatrics', admit to being worried regarding the effect of screen time 'on children's brains'. Such emotive language from experts in connection with innocent children could be expected to shock readers about the effect of using technological devices with their own children. The news that these experts support the writer's views, along with the concerned phrases 'computers should be avoided' before two years old due to the effect on a 'child's brain' and that 'children learn best by interacting with people' is intended to worry readers, jolting them upright to intently read further for a way to save their own children. The alarming phrase 'glued to screens', with its connotations of being helplessly stuck and even addicted, is designed to alarm readers who are likely to want to prevent such a fate for their own children.

Abdul raises further serious health issues associated with children's screen time. He brings up 'childhood obesity', 'eye strain', 'dehydration' and 'sleep problems' which would lead to a 'host of problems later in life'. Reading this list of horrors, concerned parents are more than likely to take any action suggested to protect their children. To ram home the seriousness of his message, the accompanying photo, of a young child with his eyes down, utterly absorbed with the screen in front of him and completely oblivious to the shelves of books in the background, is likely to appear suddenly very sinister to parents as they are shocked into thinking beyond the use of screen time as a 'substitute babysitter'. The child's fixation on the screen at the expense of other, more mentally stimulating options behind him reinforces the troubling impression created by language choices such as 'glued to screens'.

In addition to the health risks Abdul identifies, he also points out that children are at risk of bullying and unsuitable content online, encouraging parents to feel that the dangers of screens are many and varied, and that their children are therefore in dire need of protection.

Having highlighted all the reasons for which parents should be concerned about their children's screen time, Abdul returns to the strategy of admitting his own mistakes as a parent, once again easing some of the guilt and worry he has invoked in his readers. He admits to having been 'irresponsible' with his children's screen use and directly relates his own experiences and emotions to those of readers when he says, 'If this sounds anything like you, I hope you can learn from my mistakes.' By phrasing his opinion in this way, he aims to establish a bond with his audience due to shared experiences and an admission of vulnerability, thus engendering empathy and trust.

Finally, Abdul puts forward the solution he has found – limiting his children to 90 minutes of screen time a day – encouraging readers to take similar action. This also serves to alleviate their stress over screen use by providing a practical way to manage it. He leaves them with the serious message that they should 'be aware of the responsibilities' of parenting children in an age of screens, due to the wide-ranging consequences of overuse, having led them through reasoned argument, evidence and emotive appeals to their sense of guilt and protectiveness for their children to the idea that limiting screens is the best way to show this responsibility.

Sample response 17: Overtourism

Writing in the Work and Careers section of *The Australian Financial Review*, journalist Fiona Carruthers employs a lighthearted and self-critical approach to present her view on the growing issue of overtourism. Targeting an audience of well-travelled, relatively affluent Australians, she aims to encourage her readers to consider their own contribution to the problem of overtourism. Her article is accompanied by a supporting photograph.

Carruthers begins her article with an amusing anecdote about a recent hiking trip to Tasmania. She references several major famous European cities that are popular tourist destinations, presenting them as obvious examples of overtourism, which the likely well-travelled readership of *The Australian Financial Review* can potentially agree with from their own overseas experiences. Carruthers establishes a contrast between such crowded cities and her own hiking trip in 'remote Tasmania', initially positioning herself as a more considerate and aware traveller. This contrast is further reinforced by the accompanying photograph, which depicts a very crowded beach with no empty space visible. Having described herself sitting on a 'solitary dolomite rock', the implication is that she is a totally different type of traveller from the tourists depicted in the photograph and the opening paragraphs of the article. However, she then seeks to shock her readers, using statistics to highlight the huge number of tourists in Tasmania. Through this, and through reference to trendy eco-friendly items such as 'Patagonia fleeces' and 'keep cups' that her readers are likely to be familiar with and perhaps even own, she positions her audience to consider their own contribution to overtourism, and encourages them to see that they are as much to blame as city travellers, even though they might think that they are being environmentally conscious and different. By using humour to deliver this message, she hopes to charm and engage the reader and make her message – which is that they should travel less or to less popular destinations, a form of sacrifice they might find confrontational or unpleasant – more acceptable.

In the next section of her article, 'Slowing the tide', Carruthers invites readers to consider the history and causes of overtourism, along with possible solutions. She seeks to reassure readers by acknowledging it is a 'complex issue', and also identifies two modern factors – 'social media ... and low-cost travel providers' – thus suggesting that readers are not solely responsible for the problem. This again helps to make her message more palatable for readers, who are being asked to give up something that is likely to be valuable to them for the greater good. However, her use of the phrase 'we ... like to blame' subtly implies that those who are doing the blaming are not being accountable for their own actions, a message present throughout the whole of the article. Carruthers then argues that it is part of 'human nature' to travel and explore, providing a range of examples from history to support her point of view. Maintaining her humorous tone, she jokes that 'even cavemen' looked for 'better views', before providing other examples from ancient Greece, famous explorers and twentieth-century writers. Carruthers' use of a variety of examples helps her convey her point that overtourism is not new, and aims to reassure readers that their behaviour is not entirely bad. This is reinforced by the reference to 'the tide' in the section heading, as tides are inevitable and cannot be stopped, which suggests that Carruthers – and her readers – are in many ways powerless to prevent overtourism.

Having reassured her readers that their behaviour is not all bad, Carruthers gently encourages them to soften the impact they have by considering the amount they travel. She concludes her article with a focus on the 'appeal of the staycation', encouraging her audience to remain in Australia for their holidays. However, in her continued lighthearted tone, she implies that, no matter where someone might be, even within Australia, wanting to find something new is 'what us humans do'. While subtly criticising overtourism and people such as herself and her readers for not realising that they are contributing to the problem, Carruthers ultimately positions herself as a figure of fun, and challenges readers to consider whether they want to be like her. Her self-critical description as one who 'publicly lament[s] overtourism while quietly trying to get in ahead of the pack' positions readers to view her as ultimately uncaring and someone with a superficial commitment to the environment (as evidenced by the Patagonia fleece and keep cup) and to solving problems. Through this, Carruthers encourages readers to consider whether that is how they want to be viewed, or whether they would rather take actual action to reduce their impact on the problem of overtourism.

The use of subheadings reflects a 'problem and solution' structure that aids readers to follow Carruthers' argument and also allows them to see at a glance her main points, an important feature of the text given the likely busy audience she is targeting. These clear points, together with her self-deprecating tone and use of humour, all work together to present a challenging message to a potentially critical audience in a way that is likely to be easier for them to digest and hopefully act upon.

Sample response 18: Mobile phones and jaywalking

In her opinion piece, journalist Wendy Squires uses a humorous tone and a personal anecdote in her opening to draw attention to the widespread problem of wexters (pedestrians walking while using their phones). She uses informal language and personal pronouns, such as 'I was driving', 'my mate' and 'Ten bucks he won't look', to create a connection with the reader, sharing her story with them as she would with a friend. The story and the easy bet are used to lead readers to agree that such behaviour is not only predictable, but also common. The words 'the bloke … stepped … onto the road without … looking up from his phone' paint a familiar picture for readers, and this is supported by the accompanying photograph of a crowd of pedestrians looking at their phones as they walk. Their bowed heads make it look as if they are being controlled by somebody or something, and readers are likely to connect the tight grouping and trance-like appearance of people in the photograph with the idea of 'zombies' in the article's headline. Some readers would likely make a link to zombie movies where the living dead are a threat to normal living people, just as wexters are to other pedestrians and road users.

The exaggerated word choices in the headline – 'plague' and 'out of control' – with their connotations of death and chaos are used to create fear in the reader that this threatening behaviour is rapidly spreading and unchecked. Readers are led to believe that they are in danger because of these people. The writer uses strong language to label the behaviour of these pedestrians as selfish, with no regard for those around them, in order to gain support for her negative opinion of them. She claims they are 'oblivious' of others, 'self-obsessed and entitled' while 'transfixed' on their phones as if 'we simply do not exist'. The use of the word 'we' places her audience in the embattled group of normal people, like her, whose 'needs and rights' are ignored by wexters. By creating this 'us and them' dichotomy, she positions reader to want to identify with the side she places herself on, rather than with the 'selfish' wexters.

After establishing this connection, Squires introduces a more serious point about road rules and the legal offence of 'jaywalking'. She leads readers to link the behaviour of wexters with jaywalkers, through the slang definition of 'a stupid, gullible or ignorant person'. Her tone becomes more serious as she draws attention to the 10% increase in pedestrian injuries and deaths since 2010, both in Australia and overseas, caused by pedestrian distraction and disobeying road laws. She uses the 'rapidly rising' figure of '1100-plus pedestrians' injured annually on Australian roads to shock readers about the scale and danger of the problems created by wexters. This leads readers to feel alarm and dismay, and therefore makes it more likely that they will agree that strong action needs to be taken to change this behaviour.

Although Squires mentions the installation of in-ground lights at busy intersections in Melbourne and Sydney in 2016 as a measure to alert 'mobile-phone zombies' about danger ahead, she goes on to describe other more invasive government actions overseas. This aims to encourage readers to agree that more needs to be done to make pedestrians pay attention to their surroundings, in an appeal to being modern and up to date. It is designed to position readers to feel anxious about being left behind or less innovative and proactive in tackling the problem than other countries. She states it is time 'we investigate' installing the French Virtual Crash Billboards as a deterrent to wexters, because 'something needs to change … now', instilling a sense of urgency in her readers. She also returns to her humorous tone – referring to the Chinese water spraying / photo taking / facial recognition machines – in order to soften the idea of this drastic action to 'motivate wexters to concentrate' by playfully suggesting they would pay attention when walking because they would be in fear of water damage to their 'precious phones'. Thus she allows readers to both condemn the behaviour and also feel hopeful about a relatively straightforward and practical solution, which is likely to encourage them to pay attention to her message more than pessimism about the situation might.

Squires ends with another personal anecdote about her own phone behaviour. She tells the story of taking breaks from her phone every day and describes it as 'precious time' to 'unwind and rewire'. These phrases are suggestive of self-care and wellbeing, encouraging reader to associate less phone use with the positive and rewarding step of taking time for oneself, rather than depriving oneself of something. She uses this story as both a call to action and an appeal for others to change their phone behaviour and to 'turn off' so they do not turn into 'phone zombies', presenting the choice as being between selfish, foolish and dangerous behaviour, and 'carefree', positive, rewarding behaviour so that readers will be inclined to opt for the obviously preferable option.

Sample response 19: Giving gifts, not things

In a speech delivered to her extended family at a Christmas-day meal, Athena informs family members that her Christmas gifts to them are donations to charities. Adopting an overall positive tone, and appealing to family members' sense of responsibility, she argues that donating money to charity is more appropriate than material gifts.

Athena commences her speech by stating that she did not buy gifts for them. By stating her rationale, that there are 'better ways to show my love for [her] family' than giving material gifts, Athena positions family members to be supportive of the concept she is about to explain. Athena then explains that for some members, their gift is for her to complete a chore for them. By listing the examples, such as weeding the garden, sewing clothes and cooking brownies, her listeners are encouraged to be excited at receiving such benefits.

Athena then states that most of the gifts are donations to charities. Using a positive tone, by stating that she has 'chosen things that I hope will mean a lot to you' Athena wants her family members to feel content because she has considered them and their desires in the choices she has made. This presents her as kind and considerate, and thus makes it more likely that her family will empathise with her point of view. Athena then appeals to family members' social responsibility to help those less fortunate when she states, 'I think we have a duty to share some of our financial and social wealth'. By listing the ways in which they are privileged – namely with food, homes and jobs – Athena intends her family members to feel a sense of gratitude for living in a country such as Australia, and to contextualise any disappointment they may have felt in not receiving a physical gift from Athena, since many people in the world do not enjoy such a high standard of living. Athena then says, 'we have THINGS. Too. Many. Things'. The emphasis and slow pace at this point in her speech positions family members to reflect upon the fact that they have so many material possessions that they do not really need, eliciting a sense of guilt for their selfish desire for Christmas gifts.

Athena then lists other negative effects, particularly to the environment, of gift buying. She appeals to family members' environmental concerns when she asks a series of questions, such as, 'But have you thought about your carbon footprint with all that online ordering?' This positions family members to feel a sense of guilt because, through actions such as online ordering of gifts, they have contributed to global warming and damage to the environment. Athena also wants her listeners to feel guilty about the low wages and the poor treatment of the workers who made the consumer items they have purchased, when she asks, 'Do you know if they were paid fairly?' Here she implies that the workers are being denied a reasonable living wage and their exploitation is a direct result of the consumer culture in which family members participate.

Athena also argues that the practice of Secret Santa – where each member of the family agrees to buy a gift for only one other member – is flawed. By conceding that there are benefits, for example, 'it reduces the sheer volume of presents', Athena presents her argument as being reasonable and balanced. However, adopting a critical tone, she then scathingly attacks such a practice. Using words with negative connotations to describe it, such as 'greedy', 'disgusting' and 'consumerism gone mad', Athena elicits a sense of guilt from any family member who would suggest adopting a practice such as Secret Santa as an alternative to buying gifts for each family member. By saying that 'it's nothing to do with the true Christmas spirit' Athena intends family members to infer that practices which involve the routine giving of gifts are not real expressions of the Christmas spirit, and in her speech she has offered them an option that is more meaningful.

Athena ends her speech by encouraging other family members to consider adopting her course of action as an alternative to giving gifts. By stating that it is acceptable to give a gift if it is 'meaningful' or 'awesome', Athena positions family members to believe that her overall nuanced argument about gift giving is reasonable. She juxtaposes this idea against the notion that, if the gift is not really 'heartfelt, personal and meaningful … there are always other options', and, in so doing, invites family members to donate money that would be spent on gifts to charities, and feel confident in doing so. Accompanying the speech is a leaflet encouraging people to donate money to help young Victorians with mental health issues. The image of hands holding hearts symbolises the gift of love and support that the cash donation conveys, and suggests that such a donation is what Athena describes as a 'meaningful' gift. This appeal to viewers' sense of social responsibility to help those less fortunate – particularly young vulnerable people – is meant to make viewers feel inspired to donate money instead of buying gifts, and to feel positive about being able to help ease 'familial conflicts, financial crises, employment struggles' for others.

Sample response 20: Beach lessons

In her article published in *Child Monthly*, Zan Smith contends that young children need physical activity, such as playing on the beach, for their development, and expresses concern at the negative effects of overexposure to digital technology. In a thoughtful and often lyrical tone, and supported by facts, figures and references to personal experience, she shares these concerns with fellow parents of pre-school aged children, to encourage parents to ensure their children engage in adequate physical activity.

Smith begins by expressing her concern about the negative effects of overexposure to digital technology. Her anecdote at the start of the article invites the parents of pre-schoolers reading this to reflect on their own experiences of their children being 'imprisoned' indoors. The negative connotation of 'imprisoned', with its associations of people being held against their will in an environment of deprivation and hardship, underscores Smith's idea of the children being restless indoors, which positions the reader to share her frustration. Smith's concerned tone, reflected in rhetorical questions such as 'What will happen to our children when they are older…?' positions parents to feel worried about their children's development, since as parents they feel morally responsible for their children's upbringing. The reader's concern is reinforced through the first photograph showing children being mesmerised by the TV screen; the sense of being fixated is underscored by the caption 'captivated by the screen'. The question at the end of the caption, 'but how much is too much?', forces parents to wonder whether even half an hour for 'peace and quiet' is too much, and to feel a sense of worry for their children's welfare and guilt about exposing them to potential danger. The fact that the children's faces can't be seen encourages parents to imagine their own in a similar position; it also suggests the problem is general rather than specific to the writer's children.

Smith invites parents of pre-school children to share her concerns about the negative effects of insufficient physical activity through the use of statistics and research. After informing readers that children aged 8 to 18 spend hours a day watching TV and using digital devices, the writer's concerned tone, reflected in her questions, 'When do these children do their homework? Read a book? Play sport?', causes parents reading this to infer that such children lack proper cognitive and academic development, as well as physical development, positioning them to feel anxious, particularly for their own children. The series of rhetorical questions implies a long list of activities children are missing out on and aims to prompt the reader to consider other activities that might be being sacrificed to digital entertainment. Furthermore, parents are meant to share Smith's sense of 'alarm' at the rates of childhood obesity. The statement that these high rates are also ironically prevalent in Australia, with its sporting culture – 'a country where kids used to grow up playing sport' – and the figure of '27.7 % of children aged 5 to 17' being 'overweight or obese' is designed to make parents feel extremely worried, since they are unable to dismiss childhood obesity as an overseas problem. It is also an affront to national pride that the nation's children are so unhealthy, positioning readers to want to take action to improve our children's health status in relation to other countries. Furthermore, the citation of the source – the Australian Bureau of Statistics – is made to elicit parents' confidence in the validity of Smith's concern, since readers are likely to regard this as a reputable source of information.

The author also argues for the positive benefits of outdoor activity, using the beach as an example. By describing the changes in her children's behaviour from being 'cranky to content', Smith hopes to engender positive attitudes towards outdoor activities such as beach play and help readers to imagine the transformation that could be achieved in their own children. This is assisted by the photograph of the two happy children building a sandcastle, with their smiling faces, which works to engender in parents a sense of contentment, since all parents want their children to be happy and stimulated by this 'school for life'. The sunny sky and attractive beach setting help to reinforce these positive feelings and provide a stark contrast with the photo above of the children sitting passively indoors. These images thus present a choice to parents between a healthy active outdoor childhood for their children and a sedentary understimulated one indoors.

By describing these experiences as providing 'a place where children learn without even trying', with its associations of genuine development, Smith hopes to gain the reader's confidence in the benefits of outdoor activity, since all parents are likely to want their children to learn. Smith also invokes the readers' parental sense of responsibility towards their children when she compares the 'senses that aren't being engaged' when watching television to the 'sources of learning and understanding' that the outdoors offer. Parents who keep their small children indoors are meant to feel a sense of guilt, because no one wants to believe that they haven't given their children the best possible education. They are thus positioned to agree with Smith about the benefits of being outdoors, which she describes in vivid, tactile ways, such as in the phrases 'flow, absorption, textures' and 'ecstatic experience of buoyancy', designed to bring this alive for readers.

Sample response 21: Don't ban the exam

In response to suggestions that exams should be abolished for Year 12 students, Bronwyn Leigh, in her article published in *Learning Now,* contends that exams should be retained. Employing predominantly logical and conversational tones and drawing on her experience, Leigh addresses her reflections mainly to teachers and other educators.

Leigh argues that exams should be retained because they are a reliable form of assessment. She commences by using a conversational tone, reflected in the frequent use of the first person, so as to establish a rapport with her readers. This is reinforced by her reference to her own 'sleepless nights' as a result of exam panic, suggesting to the reader that she can relate to their experiences and that she understands why the very word 'exams' can evoke fear. This establishes her as honest and also somewhat vulnerable, which is intended to encourage the audience to both like and trust her.

Leigh further elicits her readers' trust – many of whom would be teachers with considerable experience – by establishing her credentials at the conclusion of the text, aiming to cement the impression of her as qualified to comment on the issue due to this. Moreover, she suggests she is taking a well-rounded and balanced view of the issue by also referring to her experience as a student. This allusion to both sides of the debate works together with her frequent acknowledgments of some of the disadvantages of exams – for example, she states that they are 'not an ideal way to assess students' – to demonstrate that she is fair in her approach and that her contention is reasonable and moderate.

By stating that she does not want exams to be the only form of assessment, Leigh presents herself as having a reasonable and balanced point of view, thus appearing to be more objective to the readers so as to gain their confidence. Leigh further reinforces this impression by acknowledging that there is 'a little merit' in criticisms of exams, thereby portraying herself as willing to see others' perspectives.

Leigh challenges the argument that exams should be abolished because some students panic and do not do well. Her assertion – that people need to be trained to deal with exam stress – is presented using a logical tone which is designed to elicit reader confidence. Leigh states that exams have been 'reliably used in education since the mid-nineteenth century', appealing to readers' sense of tradition; this framing encourages readers to question their opposition to exams; if they have been reliably used for over one hundred years, there must be merit to them. Reader confidence in examinations is solidified by Leigh comparing a student performing under examination conditions to a doctor in a hospital, as readers see the need to deal with similar stressful situations which occur in the 'real world'.

In the latter section of her article, Leigh contends that replacing an exam with a thesis is problematic. By asking the rhetorical question, 'if they were marked ... by the students' teachers, what is to stop schools from exploiting the system?' Leigh positions readers to be concerned that some students would receive favourable treatment in thesis assessment, and angry that some teachers would behave in such a way. Readers are positioned to believe that this is a violation of natural justice, contrasted against the exam, which is portrayed by Leigh as being fair. Readers are thus positioned to feel confident in the examination system; this confidence is reinforced through the photograph of the examination room. The rows of individual tables and the anonymity remind readers that in an exam all students are equal. Lastly, Leigh's assertion that 'most students do not write a formal research-based thesis until their honours year' at university attempts to provoke reader sympathy for school students, showing that it would be an unreasonable burden to place on them. Readers are thus meant to feel guilty if they support such a move because they would be forcing younger students to undertake an experience that is stressful even for adults.

Leigh's final line firmly states that exams 'should not be relegated to the dustbin of history'. This is a striking metaphor designed to alarm readers at the idea that such a familiar and long-used form of assessment might be thrown out like rubbish, disadvantaging students. 'Dustbin' has associations with waste and unpleasant substances; using this image here, after developing a reasoned and thoughtful argument for the usefulness of exams, aims to leave readers feeling that they ought to support her stance or they risk losing something valuable.

Sample response 22: Betta fish

Following her 'negative experience of buying fish in a pet shop', Rowena Soto, a mother, wrote a blog post criticising pet shops and encouraging people to stop purchasing fish from them. The post, which employs an outraged tone and relies heavily on emotive language, was published on her blog, 'EcoMums', and targeted at followers of her site, particularly those who support animal welfare. Soto also includes an image in her post to highlight the low survival rates of pet-shop fish.

Soto's outrage is clear from the beginning of her post, as she opens by recounting her recent experience at a 'chain pet shop' and her determination to never to visit one again. Including a quote from her child helps to give the scene realism and also to enhance the sympathy and shock readers are meant to feel, as the terrible plight of the fish is obvious enough to upset even a small child. Using a conversational style, she aims to treat readers as though they are her friends, as she describes the terrible conditions the Bettas were kept in, each in a 'tiny plastic cup', with 'murky water' and 'the poor fish … practically stacked on top of each other'. These descriptions are intended to appeal to the animal lovers who are reading the blog post, who are likely to agree that the conditions are cruel, and hence to think that something needs to be done to help the fish. Soto's rhetorical question, 'What are these pet shops thinking?!' is an example of a persuasive strategy she uses throughout her piece. These questions indicate her outraged amazement at the behaviour and attitudes of pet-shop owners and suggest that readers should feel similarly. Along with her critical description of the behaviour of the employees who 'shrugged' and 'had zero knowledge on caring for a Betta', this tactic aims to position readers to view the pet shop in a negative way, as a company that doesn't care properly for the animals it sells but is more concerned with making money. Readers are unlikely to want to support such an organisation or condone such a negligent attitude; thus they are positioned to agree with Soto that they should avoid buying pet-shop fish.

After attacking the employees' attitudes, Soto criticises the suitability of the products sold by the pet shop. Following her earlier alliterative description of the Bettas' conditions as 'plastic prisons', she attacks the aquariums sold for Bettas as 'disgustingly small' and laments that they could 'cause an insane amount of stress on the fish', which would potentially lead them 'to get sick and die'. These emotive descriptions target readers' sympathy by painting a worst-case-scenario image of what happens to fish in unsuitable conditions. Reader, who are likely to want animals to be well treated, are therefore positioned to listen to suggestions about how to fight against this poor treatment. Soto's exclamation that 'Fish feel pain, people!' conveys her frustration at the situation and imparts the sense of urgency she feels with regard to addressing the problem. Readers are alerted by this impassioned tone to take the issue very seriously, and to not want to be on the receiving end of Soto's anger, therefore inclining them to support her view.

Soto's argument is supported by the embedded image, which depicts the extremely high number of fish that die between capture and purchase. Fish skeletons are used to illustrate the large proportion of fish that die, while the number that survive only make up a very small part of the circle, making it clear that very few pet-shop fish survive long after capture. The accompanying statistics support the emotive illustration by suggesting the picture is based on research and evidence, promoting the reader's trust. This combination of appeals to sympathy and anger with evidence is also apparent in the written text, for example when Soto refers to her 'internet research' that she declares supports her fears about how fish are treated before they arrive at pet shops.

Soto concludes her argument with a call to action, asking 'all of [her] friends and followers' to join her in refusing to buy from pet shops. She again makes use of a rhetorical question, this time to imply that animal welfare is not a high priority for these shops. She uses language with highly negative connotations of filth and immorality – 'starve', 'rot', 'filth', 'disgust' and 'unethical' – throughout her final paragraph to reinforce the conditions of the Bettas and the feelings this provokes in her. The aim is to leave her animal-loving readers thinking about the 'poor' fish, which she presents as innocent victims of profit-seeking shops, and to position them to support her by taking action to protect the Bettas by boycotting pet shops.

Sample response 23: Bookless libraries

In response to the decline in students using print books, Petrov Price, principal of Romeo Road Secondary School, explains to parents in a blog entitled 'From the Principal's Corner' his reasons for intending to removing print books from the school library. He contends that this change is in accordance with the library's mission to provide knowledge and presents a series of reasons, based primarily on the benefits to students and their families, to support his argument.

Price begins his blog by reflecting on his childhood school library. Adopting a nostalgic tone when describing it positively – 'there was something sacred about that building' – he demonstrates to parents that he is supportive of libraries, positioning them to believe that his proposal is in accordance with the school's educational mission. Furthermore, by then describing the issue of what to do with a print book library as a set of 'difficult questions', Price presents himself as a leader who is not looking for an easy solution to complex issues; this is likely to enhance his credibility with parents. This impression of authority is enhanced by the school-branded banner under which his blog post appears, which reminds readers that he is the head of the school and gives the blog the impression of being an official and significant document. He then describes Romeo Road Secondary School as being 'at the forefront of change' since its establishment in 1945. With its positive connotations, and associations of being progressive and innovative, Price's assertion elicits parents' pride in the school, and implies that the proposal is in the best educational interests of their children. Citing the precedent of introducing PCs in the 1980s, Price intends parents to believe that the bookless library is the latest step in innovation.

Price then argues that the current library is outdated. By stating that the library is 'firmly stuck in the nineteenth' century, and by comparing the library's collection of print books to the atlas, Price positions parents to feel disdain for an institution that he presents as being counterproductive to current learning needs. This is augmented by describing a print-book library as belonging in the 'dark ages' – a negative description with associations of ignorance and superstition. Price supports his argument with the evidence that students borrowed only 45 books in the previous month, encouraging parents to believe that the books are useless, and allowing him to introduce his later argument that the space needed to house them could be better used.

Price then contrasts the advantages of a bookless library against the disadvantages of print books. He dismisses the objection in parents' mind that bookless libraries are controversial by stating that numerous libraries worldwide are phasing out physical books. By referencing the libraries 'around the world' making the change, Price encourages parents to feel confident in his proposal, positioning them to believe that if bookless libraries are becoming commonplace, Romeo Road Secondary School should also adopt this change instead of being left behind. Price then lists the benefits of a bookless library, for example, giving 'students access to more books than they have ever had before', hoping parents will have confidence in the proposal, since they are meant to believe that it will give their children access to more rather than fewer resources. Accompanying the blog is an image of a hand holding an electronic device that displays a digital library. This reinforces Price's arguments about the convenience of a digital library – namely that a greater variety of titles are available and easier to access – thereby eliciting greater parental confidence in the proposal.

Price's practical argument is enhanced by the mention of the greater space a printless library would create that could be put to better use, for example 'extra computer labs … a space for people to create things, or even a digital recording studio' – facilities parents are meant to believe would enhance their children's learning. Reinforcing his appeal to a sense of convenience, the benefits of digital books are contrasted against the negative aspects of print books that are described as 'expensive', requiring a 'significant amount of space and maintenance', eliciting a sense of disdain for them from parents. If this is not sufficient to convince parents of his view, he also offers two more supporting reasons for his stance: that bookless libraries are more hygienic and that parents will be relieved of the burden of nagging their children to return their library books. Limiting the spread of germs, particularly in a post-pandemic world, is likely to be a significant consideration for parents and again suggests that Price has students' welfare uppermost in mind. This concern is compounded by his empathy for busy parents, whom he implies he is helping by reducing their administrative workload. This contributes to the impression he gives of being wise, empathetic and caring, a characterisation intended to promote respect for his decision.

Price ends his piece by appealing to the educational needs of the children, and in doing so aims to foster rapport with parents, as he presents himself as acting in the best interests of their children.

Sample response 24: Colonising Mars

In her online article 'Three big reasons to colonise Mars – number three might surprise you!' for the website Science is Super, scientist Natasha O'Meara adopts an enthusiastic and optimistic tone to encourage her readers to agree with her argument that humans should colonise Mars because the benefits far outweigh the costs. O'Meara acknowledges concerns, which makes her seem thoughtful and reasonable, helping readers trust and agree with her. She adds to this with inclusive language (such as 'our' in the very first sentence). However, her tone is still insistent, stating throughout the article that there is no good reason not to go to Mars, instead offering three main good reasons to go. First, Earth's future is uncertain and we need a good backup. Second, we could discover alien life. Third, space exploration will involve scientific advancement that will lead to important discoveries.

O'Meara uses these three main arguments to structure her article into sections. Each argument is summarised with a numbered, bold font subheading, to make it very clear exactly what points she is making. This formatting helps avoid confusion and makes it easier for readers to accept her position, as it is set out logically and understandably. She also pairs the subheadings with direct statements explaining plainly what the article is doing: 'Here are three reasons humans should colonise Mars'. This gives her readers the best chance at understanding and therefore agreeing with her perspectives. Alongside this, she still uses a mixture of sentence lengths and some more complex language (words like 'tangible' and 'conjecture') so that her readers do not feel patronised, which might make them want to disagree. She also uses a standard register throughout, to appeal to her audience of interested but not specialist readers.

Another structuring device that helps the article flow is rhetorical questions. These are used mostly at the end of paragraphs (for example, the first and third paragraphs). The questions grab readers' attention and encourage them to keep reading (to see if O'Meara offers answers, which sometimes she does). They also subtly encourage the audience to agree with her point of view, by answering the questions in their own heads as they read. For example, she ends the article with 'So why wait?', confident that she has presented convincing arguments and reasons, so her readers will silently answer her with 'no reason!' The questions also have another purpose: they appeal to our natural human curiosity. This supports O'Meara's argument by linking to the exciting idea of space as the final frontier. The questions aim to spark readers' imaginations and desire for discovery: what she calls 'humanity's drive to push itself to its limits', elevated language that is intended to inspire the reader to support her stance.

This main reason is supported by an anecdote about the accidental invention of the microwave oven. This is a concrete illustration of O'Meara's arguments that scientific exploration is needed for 'life-changing discoveries'. It lets her readers make a personal, emotional connection: most of us use microwaves and can't imagine life without them, so if we don't go to Mars, what other 'incredible' things might we miss out on? She claims such 'advancements' are not just for 'health and wellbeing' but for 'hopes and dreams'. This poetic language connects the reader further with her arguments and aims to present colonising Mars as exciting and important. It also balances the urgency elsewhere, in emotive language such as 'necessity, a vital step'. Other figurative language includes the phrase 'wild idea', which is intended to focus the audience's attention on critics of the idea of colonising Mars by implying they are uninformed and unreasonable.

Together with these language choices, O'Meara also uses various appeals to draw on readers' existing beliefs and encourage them to agree with her. For example, she appeals to fear by highlighting the fragility of life on Earth (our existence here has only lasted 'the blink of an eye'). She quickly follows this with contrasting, reassuring language, offering a solution that will 'guarantee that the human race will endure'. This is designed to convince the reader that colonising Mars is an excellent idea. She also appeals to evidence (such as the fact of dinosaurs becoming extinct), and experts (such as popular, respected scientists Stephen Hawking and Carl Sagan) to help strengthen her arguments and suggest they are broadly supported.

The arguments are also supported by the image (placed at the beginning of the article, to help engage the reader immediately), which does two things. First, it appeals to the imagination, to excite readers: the futuristic spacesuit in the foreground is intended to conjure images of sci-fi adventures and possibility. Second, the mountain landscape in the background is not too different from a familiar Earth-scape. This is designed to make the reader feel comforted, as though colonising Mars is achievable and not frightening or too difficult. The buildings in the middle distance similarly compromise between seeming exotic enough to be tempting, yet also looking safe, to make life on Mars seem appealing. The image is also somewhat generic – we cannot see the person's face, their suit is monotone, and the foreground lacks particular features. This is intended to encourage the reader to see Mars as a blank page waiting for them to make their mark, and do whatever they like with any resources on offer. In this way the image supports O'Meara's argument that Mars should be colonised.

Sample response 25: Vegan shoes

In his article titled 'If you think your Vegan shoes are saving the planet, you're wrong', writer Tanner Bowden discusses his perspective on some of the potential issues with vegan shoes. Bowden adopts a humorous and conversational tone to target an audience who are interested in leading an ethical life, arguing that vegan shoes are not always the more ethical alternative.

Bowden begins the article with the use of the phrase 'I have beef', a play on the commonly used term that takes on an ironic twist given the context of the article. By making this play on words, Bowden immediately attempts to establish a conversational, lighthearted tone for his piece. This is intended to avoid creating a tone of superiority and turning the piece into a lecture; Bowden aims to avoid moralising or lecturing, as the audience of the environmentally conscious lifestyle magazine he is writing for is likely to have a number of vegan members, and adopting too critical a tone could potentially alienate these readers.

Bowden immediately proceeds to extol the virtues of vegans, explaining that he thinks 'vegans are heroes' and that their decision to avoid animal products 'is literally saving the world'. He reiterates that he doesn't have any issues with vegans and that he has even tried going vegan himself. By doing so, Bowden attempts to frame himself as sympathetic towards and understanding of vegans, encouraging his audience to view his position as balanced and well thought out. This is also intended to avoid alienating or upsetting his audience, who are likely to be either vegan themselves or at least supportive of the idea. By stating that his problem is with vegan shoes specifically, Bowden seeks to reassure the audience that his concerns are environmental in nature, rather than stemming from any prejudice against vegans. This is reinforced later in the piece by Bowden's direct address of the reader: 'If lessening animal cruelty is the primary motivation behind your veganism'. This makes Bowden's intent to target the piece at a vegan or vegan-friendly audience explicit. Bowden also continues to maintain a conversational rapport with the reader throughout.

Bowden then proceeds to explain his argument; that, despite perceptions to the contrary, vegan leather shoes are not actually more environmentally sustainable than the alternative. He references the materials these shoes are sometimes made of – polyvinyl chloride and polyurethane. The use of this scientific jargon is intended to add credibility to Bowden's argument by framing him as an expert on the topic with an understanding of the mechanics of vegan leather production beyond that of the average person. Bowden also appeals to his readership base's consciousness of the environment by comparing vegan leather shoes to 'the cheap plastic-and-foam flip flops that wash up on beaches'. By doing so, Bowden seeks to reframe the idea of vegan leather as inherently sustainable, comparing it to the obviously environmentally damaging litter that ends up on beaches. This is reinforced by his reference to the 'harmful chemicals' used in the production of vegan leather. The phrase implies danger and aims to evoke alarm in the reader in order to position them to feel sceptical of vegan leather.

Bowden then references the vegan brand OluKai, citing their acknowledgement of the issue. He points out that the company itself states that 'animal-free shoes are not always more "environmentally friendly"'. By using evidence from a manufacturer of vegan leather shoes, Bowden seeks to appeal to authority to reinforce his argument; it is intended to make the reader think that even producers of vegan leather shoes understand and agree with him. This is further emphasised by Bowden's reference to companies that 'greenwash over such nuance', implying that OluKai are trustworthy because they admit that there are issues with vegan leather and, by extension, so is Bowden himself. The use of the term 'greenwashing', a common term among the environmentally conscious, is also intended to frame Bowden as part of that community, thereby encouraging readers to listen to what he has to say.

Bowden continues to maintain a personal tone throughout the piece, relaying an anecdote about his experiences in New York. Bowden uses the anecdote to portray himself as personally familiar with the problems seemingly ethically motivated decisions and policies can present. Together with his personal tone, it also contributes to the rapport he has been trying to develop with the reader from the outset of the piece.

Bowden concludes by discussing the ways in which both real and faux leather production is becoming more environmentally sustainable. He focuses particularly on real leather production, encouraging his readers to view it as the more sustainable alternative. He references Patagonia, a well-known retailer, appealing to its name-brand status to incline readers to trust it and, by extension, him. He also uses a range of language with positive connotations of environmental sustainability, such as 'restores the grasslands' and 'promotes carbon sequestration'. This language is intended to encourage readers interested in environmental sustainability to at least consider switching from faux to real leather products, and frames Bowden as invested in and knowledgeable about environmental issues.

The article is accompanied by an image that portrays a pair of vegan leather shoes, as well as the ingredients used in their production. The shoes are placed in the background of the image and are not completely in focus. In contrast, the mushroom mycelium and vegan bio leather are in the foreground and immediately draw the reader's eye. This framing suggests that vegan shoes themselves are not the issue and not what readers should be focusing their attention on; rather, the materials and context of their production are what readers should be concerned about. This supports the article's contention, which focuses on the sustainability issues involved in producing vegan shoes. The shoes are obscured by the ingredients, and are partially in the shadow of the vegan leather, again focusing the reader's attention on the production process rather than the end product.

Acknowledgements

Insight Publications thanks the following writers for their contributions to this resource: Laken Ballinger, Anica Boulanger-Mashberg, Niki Cook, Michael E Daniel, Sage Napthine-Morrison, Tess Rooney, Alison Tealby, Mariano Trevino.

Insight Publications is also grateful to the following individuals and organisations for permission to reproduce copyright material.

Fiona Carruthers and *The Australian Financial Review* for 'Overtourism: why you're the one to blame'

Wendy Squires and *The Sydney Morning Herald* for 'The jaywalking phone zombie plague is completely out of control'

Tanner Bowden and *Gear Patrol* for 'If you think your vegan shoes are saving the planet, you're wrong'

Images by Melisa Paredes and Gisela Beer. Other images from iStock and Shutterstock.